W9-BBA-810

GIFTS FROM HILDEGARD

By the same author

At Ease With Stress
People Need Stillness
Christ, Stress and Glory

GIFTS
FROM HILDEGARD

Wanda Nash

**Illustrated by
Sister Mary Stephen
Grindon-Welch CRSS**

DARTON·LONGMAN + TODD

First published in 1997 by
Darton, Longman and Todd Ltd
1 Spencer Court
140–2 Wandsworth High Street
London SW18 4JJ

ISBN 0–232–52212–X

A catalogue record for this book is available from the British Library.

Designed by Sandie Boccacci
Phototypeset in Sabon by Intype London Ltd
Printed and bound in Great Britain by
Page Bros, Norwich

For Michael Hollings, who companioned so many of us along the way;

> for whom background, age, churchmanship, gender, and status was of little interest;
> for whom Love and Joy in God were living glories.
> Thanks be to God.

And for Astrid and Brigid, who understand what it is to suffer and to glorify.

CONTENTS

INTRODUCTION
AND CONSTRUCTION OF THIS BOOK

The train was late, and a small group of us were meandering along the nearby canal filling in time. 'Would you like to lead a weekend on Hildegard?' she said. That brought me up short. Certainly I had picked up a few phrases from 'popular' books on spirituality, and used them to bolster my own argument whenever I lead prayer groups; but this was a challenge to home in on the *real* Hildegard of Bingen . . . This was a totally different matter.

So I deflected a direct answer, and promised to think about it.

Back at home, I ferreted about for the various bits from Hildegard which I had stored from anthologies. Together they added up to an insufficiency that was tantalising. So I took on an exploration of the whole translated works, and I was hooked. The compulsion was born to share such treasures as these with others.

Two years on, I have in mind modern readers who have limited time, and who are faced with competing demands from all sides, all clamouring for their attention. So my aim has been to devise a way in which such readers can grasp the most relevant of Hildegard's ideas, while also providing various opportunities to fill them out at greater depth.

The construction of the book is such that it can be used in any of several ways:

- Sometimes readers may be wanting a 'quick dip' into Hildegard's thinking; in this case they can focus on the material printed on *every right-hand page.*
- Sometimes readers may be wanting to see how Hildegard's words
  - resonate with the teaching of other spiritual writers,
  - or they may be looking for some contextual comment,
  - or some further expansion from Hildegard herself,
  - or they may wonder how her ideas reflect on their everyday lives.
  - Such issues as these are printed on the *left-hand pages.* Every 'theme' section contains at least one page of each of these issues.
- Sometimes the reader will want simply to stay with the illustration of the theme, those drawn so profoundly by Sister Mary Stephen; perhaps this is most appropriate after the words have been read already, and as an aid to meditating upon them.
- Some readers will use the entire book as a study, in addition to simply

enjoying its contents. For these, sources have been detailed very precisely, and a list of selected further reading has been provided as well as where to follow up other quotations used.

It has been shown that our eyes tend to look first at the right-hand page of any double page spread, and so the genuine sounds of Hildegard have been placed on the pages to the right. The left pages catch some echoes of her ideas. It can be a temptation to become nostalgic and to sentimentalise what she says, to attempt to make it fit in with what we *want* her to have said. To do so carries the risk of losing her startling originality; maybe the 'echoes' will reinforce the clarity of her true voice.

Hildegard dictated, by word, the visual interpretations of her spiritual insights. These are known as her 'illuminations' and have been published widely. Our aim for this book was to find an artist with the courage and commitment to take on the task of visually resonating with her words in a modern idiom. We are thrilled to be favoured with the skill and perception of the one who took up the work. Sister Mary Stephen was born in Berkshire and from her earliest childhood was exposed to things that were of greatest significance to Hildegard. Her mother was deeply interested in agriculture – 'green-ness' – while her father was equally drawn to education – 'speculative knowledge'. She studied art at Reading University, then in Belgium, and at Swansea; she has been responsible for the setting up and development of a large Art Department at New Hall in Boreham, Essex. For many years Sister Mary Stephen's pictures have been valued locally and in her community's spirituality outreach; I am proud to be associated with her illustrations to this book as her work deservedly reaches a wider public.

As to the words themselves, Hildegard insisted to her contemporaries that when she interpreted her visions she did not speak with her own voice, her own self. The images and language came directly from God, and she was simply the pot or vessel to be filled, a feather being blown by the wind, a lyre with strings being played by a breeze from God. The writing of her letters and lyrics is of a somewhat different character: it tends to be more personal and immediate. Two of Hildegard's favourite virtues are moderation and discretion, but when her concern is for a particular cause or individual her language becomes extravagant. In the following pages there are selections from both types of her expression.

A prime construct to Hildegard is *usefulness*, seen by her as enthusiasm tempered by 'rationality'. The present book is not intended to provide some sort of quaint sideglance at what has been; much more, Hildegard's themes enable us to face up to some of the deepest revelations of Christ-centred belief, most particularly those which have been sidetracked in our passionate search for comfort. She doesn't take to trivialisation of great matters, she won't allow for the levelling we see daily in our modern culture. You will find some of her ideas disturb you, if you are prepared to absorb what she is saying. But if Hildegard's message adds depth to the usefulness we make of our daily living, the book will have proved its own usefulness. Please God it does.

OVERVIEW

It could be said that the centuries which cradled the life of Hildegard were the pivot of the Middle Ages. Just as 1066 marked a unique turning-point in the history of Britain, so in Europe the culture was stretched by a wave of new challenges. As the tumult of the rampaging Vikings came to be seen as a thing of the past, monasteries expanded in wealth and influence. The arts themselves drew from a new sense of excitement, and into the previously drab greyness of life there was an injection of vibrancy and colour.

It was an age of enormous contrasts. Let's imagine some of them:

- Rich merchants and most of the nobility luxuriated; they lived surrounded by silks and spices and artefacts traded from areas across deserts, over mountainous wildernesses and through wild seas – at huge cost to life and limb. Yet just outside the gates of their mansions the streets ran with putrifying sewerage and the poor scrabbled for a livelihood in horribly overcrowded alleys. Those living there had neither clean water, nor a change of clothing, nor access to the most basic knowledge of healthcare.
- It was a time when well-educated monks could be indulged with sophisticated and passionate theology; but the common people were left struggling with a swamp of rampant superstition.
- In the cities, music and art flourished; courtly behaviour and dancing were the models of the day. But in the countryside, most of the land was shrouded in primeval forest.
- At that time, sex was robust and lewd: women were expected to be pregnant annually. But miscarriage was common, and not even half the babies born survived into their third year.
- It was a time when the rich, particularly the rich young men, travelled around Europe and further afield to drink in culture and education; yet the poor could neither read nor write. Learning was tied up in precious manuscripts that were hand-copied, and kept in secluded book-rooms. Even those that were accessible were not written in a familiar or indigenous language, but in Latin.
- There was a great thirst for the performance of heroic deeds. Story-telling was the universal 'leisure pursuit', and those who added to the stock of familiar tales of heroism were immediately popular. This greed for heroism went horrifically awry in the records of the Crusades. Church and secular

leaders alike approved of those who risked everything they had, who sacrificed their homes, lands, and families to take up the challenge of joining 'Christian' hordes crossing Europe to 'rescue' the lands of the Bible from the infidels. The atrocities committed in the name of Christ have yet to be matched for their ingenuity and ferocity; yet these appalling feats were undertaken from a position seen as the heroic high ground.

It was into this melee of contrasts that Hildegard was born. All around her the ordinary experience of ordinary people bred fear and rage, jealousy and reprisal, bawdiness and bewilderment. Sometimes these powerful emotions would break out in the market-place, but any skirmish there would soon be squashed by the feudal laws of punishment. This powerful civic control, added to the moral security which comes with each person 'knowing their place', kept revolution at bay for another few centuries. In this climate, those who yearned for change did so at the metaphysical and mystical level; practical politics still lay in the future.

Hildegard grew up in such a climate of contrast and repression; yet she was to become the first woman in Europe to write books, the first woman to admonish and moralise in public, the first female to compose and disseminate music, and the first to collect and publish data concerning things of the body. All in direct opposition to the accepted male dominance.

At the court of the Count of Spandau,[1] as in any of the land-owning courts, the women were expected to be mild and languid, decorative and obedient. The menfolk could do extreme things like go to war, or opt out of family life and take to the priesthood. The obligation on priests to celebrate mass daily meant they had to remain celibate for the previous twenty-four hours. Therefore they lived without wives. Of those who went to war, hand-to-hand battles were bloody and mutilating. Few returned able-bodied. The number of eligible young men were few, and they were insufficient to match the numbers of marriageable daughters. Well-bred young girls had to be protected from the contamination of personally-chosen relationships, and trade, and alien influences, so, conveniently, their fathers enclosed them in religious orders. This arrangement had many advantages for the patriarchal heads of the great families: not only would the souls and bodies of their daughters be kept out of the way of harm and put on the way to salvation, but the prayers they offered would make up for the lack of sanctity of their male relatives.

And so it came about that when a knight at the court of Count Spandau proclaimed that his tenth child, a little girl named Hildegard, had started seeing visions at the age of six, she was taken by her family and put under the protection of a newly refounded monastery at Disibodenberg. This was in the Rhineland of what is now known as Germany. The Count had a sister, Jutta, who was living as a female hermit attached to the monastery. She was pious and pure and the eight-year-old Hildegard was put into her care. These two were literally walled into two small rooms attached to the abbey church, preceded by a religious rite which reflected their death to the world. They would have had attendants to see to their daily needs, but between them they led a totally secluded life, reading psalms, praying the Benedictine daily offices, and doing some small handicrafts. As time went on, a number of select devout ladies joined them, and the buildings to accommodate them grew. At fifteen years old, Hildegard took her vows as a fully habited nun.[2]

The intense spiritual visions continued, but because they came to a woman, they were considered to be of no consequence and Hildegard held them to herself. She must have felt at times like exploding with the power of the messages with which she believed she had been entrusted. By her own account, the repression which was the result of this holding back led to frequent and extensive periods of debilitation and severe pain. She was laid low and invalided by weakness and 'countless grave sufferings'[3] which were 'so intense I was unable to sit up'.[4] In the first letter that she wrote to an ecclesiastic for help, she says, 'I am wretched and more than wretched in my existence as a woman. Gentle father, you are so secure, answer me, your unworthy servant girl, who from childhood has never, not even for one single hour, lived in security.'[5] Nevertheless, the number of pious ladies drawn to her company increased, and in 1136, at the age of thirty-eight, Hildegard succeeded Jutta van Spanheim as the abbess of the community of Benedictine nuns now attached to the Disibode monastery. Eventually she established a fully developed convent, and the monks thrived on the attention which her writings and her music brought to them.

Initially the writings were done in order to uplift her nuns. But when Hildegard reached the age of forty-three, she received a strong command from God to 'write and tell' of her visions. Diffidently and somewhat secretively she made use of the services of a sympathetic monk, called Volmar, to transfer her insights to permanent form. At first they were discounted by the leaders of her home monastery. When Abbot Bernard, famous for his reforms of the great Cistercian abbey at Clairvaux, saw them he recommended them to the Trier Synod. Hildegard took courage and began to acknowledge her own spiritual strength more publicly. Later even Pope Eugenius III gave his approval to her writings, and it is as though the dammed-up energy of three and a half decades broke loose. Hildegard could no longer hold back, and images in words and music and illumination came flooding out of her.

By the end of the 1140s Hildegard was determined to break away from the strangling protection of Disibodenberg. The monks were dismayed; her move would end all the increase of honour and dowries that her presence had brought. They put up all sorts of delaying tactics. Hildegard stuck to her plans, and in spite of considerable blocking in 1150 the whole convent of nuns moved out from under the authority of the abbey and into the buildings of a deserted community site across the river. This place was known as Rupertsberg, and it was close to the town of Bingen. The inspirited nuns took on the construction themselves, and from this revitalised convent Hildegard's influence grew. In time, under her guidance, a mixed monastery of monks and nuns developed, and among those professed were one of her own sisters and two of her brothers.

The list of books, anthems and treatises composed by Hildegard grew. She wrote on theology, ethics, herbalism and early medical cures, physiology, biography, poetry and music. Her knowledge and interests were extra-ordinarily wide. She was in great demand as a popular preacher, and her advice was sought by secular and spiritual leaders alike. Her letters to royal houses – including that of England – became a byword, and she even remon-strated with the Pope. In days when travelling was full of danger and great dis-comfort, she travelled from Rupertsberg right through Europe encouraging and admonishing the Church hierarchy right in the face of their male privileges.

The most remarkable aspects of Hildegard's story is the manner in which a private, hemmed in, 'tiny spark' of a young woman becomes so charged by the message she hears from God that she dominates the scene of recrimination wherever she finds it necessary. Popes, kings, abbots; queens, nuns, fellow-mystics: where encouragement is needed she offers it, but where criticism is appropriate she is fearless in handing it out, believing them to be 'exiles, who do not recognise what is heavenly'. She likens herself to a trumpet which allows the sound through – sometimes weakly – but insists that she is not herself the source of the sound.[6] Further, she says: 'God always disciplines those who blow God's trumpets, and God sees to it that the earthen vessel does not break'.[7]

Hildegard was familiar with personal repression and – later – public adu-lation. Few of us today, even with all our change and conflict, can get inside the extraordinary dynamics of this remarkable woman. It is difficult for us, as we launch into the twenty-first century, to grasp fully the astonishing power of the gifts of Hildegard, breaking through the constraints and inhibitions of her time. None the less we can join in with her and be enriched by her sonorous, exulting, life-affirming love of God. A list of Hildegard's major works is to be found on p. xxix, following this Overview.

Hildegard's Written Language

'But you, O tiny soul, speak about the fiery work'.

As far as scholars can tell, the young Hildegard soon gave up putting her own words down on wax tablets. She had little confidence in her command of Latin grammar and construction (with good reason!) and she enlisted the help of professional scribes with greater skills.[8] Her daily work required her to read German and Latin, but in her correspondence she insists to Bernard of Clairvaux that she has 'received no schooling'.[9] The language in which she received her visions was 'in an unknown language yet to be heard, not in the ordinary human forces of expression'. The scribe Volmar, a monk who became a confidant and friend, was sent as 'a file, to eagerly smooth this speech so it receives the right sound for human ears'.[10] The illuminations were also dictated to Volmar in word-form, and we have no evidence of Hildegard being an artist herself. Many of these have a small insert of a picture of Hildegard holding a wax tablet, and receiving a beam of inspiration directly from above. Totally unlike the modern word processor which is so general today, these wax tablets had no means of altering or editing the script which was drawn onto them. Her works were then copied by hand onto parchment in the monastery Scriptorium, and the evidence of these manuscripts is that at this stage they were corrected and the corrections recorrected, by others.[11]

It has to be admitted that most of the writings could well have benefited from the red pen of an astute copy-editor. At times her meaning is obscured through over-long elaborated sentences, repetition of ideas, and abstract illogicality. This seems inevitable if she did not have the means to reconsider or alter what she had spontaneously dictated. At times, the explications and extrapolations which Hildegard draws out of a single vision take up a hundred chapters.[12] When this vocabulary and phraseology is translated into English, the results are extraordinarily original. The excitement they generate must derive from Hildegard's first instructions – in no other way could they have survived the sequence of translations from:

- spiritual vision
- into verbal mother-tongue expression
- into Latin

– into German
– into English.

It is the overall themes that make us hold our breath, awed anew by the startlement of a fresh insight. Let me give you an immediate example:

> And Truth Spoke:
> I want to be like a green twig to be used ... as a scourge against that deceitful one who is the son of the devil. I am contrary and irksome to the devil. I spit the devil out of my mouth, like a deadly poison even though the devil has never entered me. I trample the devil underfoot with the justice of God, which is unendingly lovable to me.[13]

Hildegard's Theological Context

Like the Celtic saints before her – and in many ways they were her philosophical forerunners – Hildegard's influence stretched out beyond her geographical boundaries to solace, sustain, and admonish both those who were her soul-friends and the non-converted; but like the Celtic saints she drew on a central community life for her own spiritual strength. Her first monastic home, Disibodenberg, had been built on a site of pre-Christian worship, recovered by a Celtic missionary saint. This monk, named Disibod, came from Ireland or Scotland and lived there as a hermit in the seventh century. Later, Hildegard was to write a biographical reconstruction of his life.

Looking at the prolific total of Hildegard's writing, we have to remember the context from which they were produced.

(a) The community of professed women whom Hildegard led had been taught to think of themselves in terms of frailty and timidity in comparison with men.[14] In their contemporary theological culture, it was assumed that self-subjugation on the part of the sisters was rewarded by

  (i) the approval of, though not necessarily the attention of, the monks living in the main abbey; and

  (ii) the accumulation of merit in heaven.

  It was these nuns for whom Hildegard yearned to raise the concept of self-worth in the eyes of God, however fragile and penitential they felt themselves to be.

(b) Similarly, the theology of her time expressed a strong conviction of the process of dualism. It commonly took the form of:

  light\dark;   good\evil;   virginity\concupiscence.

Hildegard supports this doctrine wholeheartedly. She says, 'You are of heaven in the spirit, of the earth in the flesh'.[15] But she also expresses a strong belief that the negative *serves* the positive. This is often referred to, and is typified by the following:

> God made His splendour rise over the filth: and that splendour shone with great brightness, as that filth stank exceedingly. The sun gleamed forth in its brightness, and the filth putrefied in its foulness: and therefore the sun was embraced by those beholding it with much greater love than if the filth had not been there opposite it.[16]

(c) Since the third century, Augustinian teaching had extolled virginity as being the highest of all virtues and brightest of all crowns in God's sight. It was seen as an offering to Him close in value to that of martyrdom. Hildegard herself wrote that marriage and procreation can be tolerated, because some of the ensuing offspring may become virgins. Later, she extends this toleration even more: 'Married people, if faithful, can hold fast their desire for heaven even though they are still begetting children.'[17] While she urges such 'toleration' for those who are married, she keeps her most fulsome praise for those who are virgins; nevertheless she remains scathing towards people who 'tepidly keep their bodies intact from fornication, but reject the virginity of the Spirit . . . They have lived neither in the flesh nor in the Spirit'.[18]

(d) All of Hildegard's work was set to the background of the continuing Crusades. The peculiar piety of the crusaders and the Knights Hospitallers, which embraced such fervent compulsions and such illogical drives, is never directly mentioned, but much of the current phraseology concerning battles, defeat, warfare and triumphalism is imaged repeatedly in her writings. The spiritual direction she received from Bernard of Clairvaux embraced those who left everything behind in order to follow the Crusades, but Hildegard herself found all aspects of war reprehensible. This was in direct contrast with the Christian thinkers of her time.

Resonance with Modern Thinking

(i) Hildegard's reverence for the whole of the created universe was quite out of the ordinary, most particularly for her historical period. For instance, she proclaims:

> The rest of creation cries out and complains loudly . . . because the more vile human nature is, the more it is a rebel gainst God.
> The rest of creation fulfils the commandments of God with fear and reverence.

The rest of creation cries aloud above or over mankind, with the crashing of sounds ... for it is *spread over mankind*.[19]

(ii) Although she remains a woman of her day in her severe judgements against those who sin and the ease with which the devil can divert people into his blackness, the degree to which Hildegard pursued and enlarged the then contemporary understanding of physicality was prophetic. She was the first to write maturely of the qualities of herbs and elements, of the physiological connections within the human body, and of the remedies that could be used to good effect to bridge the two. She is never reticent in her descriptions of sexuality, and the crucial emotional as well as the physical differences between women and men.

(iii) At all times, Hildegard remains securely a woman of her time in her exaltation of virginity and celibacy, but her desire to increase the self-understanding of her nuns, and their sense of self-worth, is tireless. In this she was centuries ahead. She wrote homilies to edify their thinking, health advice to improve their physical strength, biographies and explanations, and answers to questions to ease their mental confusion.

The Gifts of Hildegard Applicable to Us Today

With modern high technology the music of Hildegard is reaching a growing and devoted audience. Her unambivalent purity and the serenity of her intentions towards God are of supreme solace to us in our frenetic materialism. At times, the theology she expresses in her lyrics may not be to our modern taste, but the exquisite and innovative way in which she uses the vocal musical modes of her day can feed us in our search towards single-mindedness.

Our immediate concern is with her writings, and here we do well to guard against the temptation of reinterpreting what is actually stated in Hildegard's work in order to match what it is we want her to say about our modern attitudes to life. There are some things that stand out above any controversy.

Hildegard is unequivocal. For all her gifts – and she could have made her name as poet, musician, herbalist, visionary, adviser, administrator, diplomat, traveller – *God came first*. Hers was not a message of mushy consolation. Second-best was never good enough for Hildegard. God is always primary. In praising God Hildegard was triumphal. She rang all the bells there are, in words, music, poetry, illustration, healing and building. This book makes a selection of some of these gifts Hildegard has to give us. She has insights for our present experience on things like:

– today's gluttony for experience;

- our modern popularity for individualism;
- the way in which we continually drain each other dry;
- the manner of our materialism;
- our insistent exploitation of the created things around us;
- the idea that I am here to make use of the things to hand, in contrast with the idea that I am here to prove my 'usefulness' to God.

More, Hildegard has gifts to offer us which relate to our modern convictions of personal superiority and intellectual strength. For instance, in

• our superiority in deriding the personalisation of the devil;
• our superiority in claiming we can do it on our own; and
• our superiority in our addiction to self-sufficiency.

Perhaps most of all, she offers us a deep underlying reassurance in today's perplexing world. In spite of all her proclamations, and her defiance of authority and condemnation of everything she saw as evil, Hildegard remained in touch with her true, inner, fault-full self. In a letter to one of her closest friends, Elisabeth of Schöngau, she says: 'But even I, who suffer from a heart of little courage and am again and again disturbed and crippled by fear, even I sometimes sound with a weak note from the trumpet of the living light. May God help me to persevere in divine service.'[20] And so say all of us.

The selections from Hildegard's writing which are in this book have been chosen for their inherent authenticity, and also because they are each characteristic of her thinking. It is her way to reiterate her main themes constantly, right through all her works, so although the greater number of quotations come from *Scivias*, these ideas continue in her later writing, often in an elongated form.

Finally
Hildegard writes about our 'panting and thirsting' for God,

> scaffolded by virtues
>> fortressed by good works
>>> journeying with steadfastness through trials, showers of arrows
>>> and temptations, towards the eternal brightness of God.

Overarching all is her conviction of the present and eternally ongoing glory of God, and the 'salivic efficiency' of the incarnation of His Word.

It may be that not all of Hildegard's words and ideas speak directly to you and your own circumstances today; but there can be no doubt that her

---

originality, profundity, and imagination will catch you unawares and bolster your faith – or they will challenge you to answer *why* it doesn't.

As Hildegard herself concludes one of her letters:

> O Son of God, your life is like the earth which brings forth both useful plants and useless weeds ... When pride attacks you, ... so that you consider yourself wiser and more trustworthy than others, and all their doings thereby displease you ... then remember that you are capable of nothing without the grace of God ... Then the enemy, conquered by you, will howl in its shame and God will rejoice in you and make you God's chosen and beloved dwelling place.[21]

Most important of all, please enjoy the book.

Notes

Key to abbreviations of main sources is to be found on pp. xxix–xxx

1. Also spelt Spanheim.
2. See SCc for expanded details of Hildegard's early life.
3. See DWe, p. 5.
4. DWe, p. 272.
5. DWe, p. 271.
6. DWe, p. 340.
7. DWe, p. 340, letter to Elisabeth of Schöngau.
8. See Albert Derolez, 'The Genesis of Hildegard of Bingen's "Liber Divinorum Operum" – the Codicological Evidence', in Gumbert and Haan (eds.), *Litterae Textuales* Vol. 2, Van Gendt, Amsterdam, 1972, pp. 23–33.
9. SCc, p. 128.
10. DWe, p. 276: from a letter to Pope Anastasius IV.
11. See note 7 above.
12. See DWf, p. 62.
13. SCa, p. 243: 3.V6.4 (contracted).
14. E.g. *Scivias* 3.V10.7; 3.V10.27; many letters; DWf; and B. Newman in Nichols and Shank (eds.) *Peace Weavers*, Cistercian Publications Inc., 1987.
15. SCa, p. 322: 3.V10.3.
16. SCb, p. 88: 1.V2.32.
17. SCa, p. 174: 2.V7.25.
18. SCb, p. 478: 3.V10.8.
19. SCa, p. 236: 3.V5.17 (compacted).
20. DWe, p. 340.
21. DWe, p. 347: letter to an unknown lay person (compacted).

CONTEXT OF MEDIEVAL WRITERS

	Men	*Women*
1033–1109	St Anselm of Canterbury	
1079–1142	Peter Abelard (France)	with Heloise
1090–1153	St Bernard of Clairvaux	
1085–1148	William of Thierry	
1096–1141	Hugh of St Victor (France)	
1098–1179		*Hildegard of Bingen*
1110–1167	Aelred of Rievaulx (Yorkshire)	
1123–1175	Richard of St Victor	
1182–1226	St Francis of Assisi	
1217–1282		Mechtild of Magdeburg
1225–1274	Thomas Aquinas (Italy)	
1240–1298		Mechtild of Hackeborn
1248–1309		Angela of Foligno (Umbria)
1251–1291		Gertrude of Hackeborn
1256–1301		Gertrude the Great (Germany)
1260–1327	Meister Eckhart (Germany)	
1295–1366	Henry Suso (Germany)	
1300–1361	John Tauler of Strassburg	
1300–1396	Walter Hilton (England)	
1300–1349	Richard Rolle (England)	
1303–1307		Bridget of Sweden
1342–1420		Dame Julian of Norwich
1379–1471	Thomas à Kempis (Germany)	

late fourteenth century, Anon: *The Cloud of Unknowing*

Approximate date of publication:

1149 *Scivias – Know the Ways*, completed. This large volume includes 36 illuminations, as well as the earliest liturgical morality play yet to be discovered: *Ordo virtutum* – the Play of the Virtues. This last was set to music.

1150 Following the move of the convent to Rupertsberg, a large ecclesiastical correspondence developed. Some of this has survived.

1152 *Liber simplicis medicinae* – a book of natural history, and *Liber compositae medicinae* – a manual on medicine.

1158 *Physica* – the Book of Simple Medicine

1158 *Causae et curae* – the Book of Compound Medicine

1163 *Liber vitae meritorium* – the Book of Life's Merits

1173 *Liber divinorum operum* – the Book of the Divine Works. Also called *De operatione Dei* – On the Activity of God.

In addition:

Symphonia harmoniae celestium revelationum – Symphony of the Harmony of Celestial Revelations in seventy sequences and hymns for her community.

Vita Sancti Disibodi – the life of St Disibod

Vita Sancti Ruperti – the life of St Rupert

Solutiones Triginta – answers to 38 questions for her nuns

Explanatio Symboli S. Athanasii – explanation of St Athanasius

Explanatio Regulae S. Benedicti – commentary on the Rule of St Benedict

Expositio Evangeliorum – addresses relating to the Gospels

50 allegorical homilies

Lingua ignota; Litterae ignotae – discussing her own invented language 'for her diversion' – of 900 words and an alphabet of 23 letters.

145 letters have been preserved and printed, addressed to 4 popes, 2 emperors, cardinals, kings – including Henry II of England and his queen Eleanor ('Beware of flattery, unrest, and inconstancy'), religious of all ranks, and ordinary men & women.

KEY TO THE MAIN SOURCES

The words of Hildegard are drawn from a number of different tranyslations, each of which can be identified using the following abbreviations.

Scivias:

SCa *Hildegard of Bingen's Scivias*, by Hozeski, copyright 1986, Bear & Co., Santa Fe, New Mexico; translator: Hozeski.

SCb *Hildegard of Bingen: Scivias*, by Hart & Bishop, copyright 1990, Paulist Press, Mahwah, New Jersey; translators: Mother Columba Hart and Jane Bishop.

SCc *Hildegard of Bingen: an Anthology*, edited by Fiona Bowie and Oliver Davies, copyright 1990, SPCK, London; translator: Robert Carver.

SCd *Illuminations of Hildegard of Bingen*, by Matthew Fox, copyright 1985, Bear & Co., Santa Fe, New Mexico, main translators: A. Fuhr-Kotter (Turnhaut, 1978) and Schipperges (Salzburg, 1965).

Book of Divine Works:

DWe *Hildegard of Bingen's Book of Divine Works, with Letters and Songs*, edited by Matthew Fox, copyright 1987, Bear & Co., Santa Fe, New Mexico; translator: Robert Cunningham.

DWc *Hildegard of Bingen: an Anthology*, edited by Fiona Bowie and Oliver Davies, copyright 1990, SPCK, London; translator: Robert Carver.

DWf *Hildegard of Bingen: A Visionary Life*, by Sabina Flanagan, copyright 1989, Routledge, NY & London; translator: Sabina Flanagan.

Book of Life's Merits:

LWc *Hildegard of Bingen: an Anthology*, edited by Fiona Bowie and Oliver Davies, copyright 1990, SPCK, London; translator: Robert Carver.

Letters:

Le *Hildegard of Bingen's Book of Divine Works, with Letters and Songs*, edited by Matthew Fox, copyright 1987, Bear & Co, Santa Fe, New Mexico; translator: Ronald Miller.

Anthems and Songs:

Ac   *Hildegard of Bingen: an Anthology,* edited Fiona Bowie and Oliver Davies, copyright 1990, SPCK, London; translator: Robert Carver.

Ae   *Hildegard of Bingen's Book of Divine Works, with Letters and Songs,* edited by Matthew Fox, copyright 1987, Bear & Co, Santa Fe, New Mexico; translators: Rev. Jerry Dybdal and Matthew Fox.

Ag   *Heart of Love: Prayers of German Women Mystics,* Brian Pickett, 1991, St Paul Publications UK; translator: Brian Pickett.

New translations by Brian Pickett are attributed individually.

Additional symbols:
* indicates an extract which has been contracted
\# indicates an extract which has been compacted.

Theme One:

Approaching the Creator

Illustration overleaf:
*The circle shone its brightness forth – the brightness spread itself upward to the
height of heaven and downward to the depth of the abyss.*

HIS BRIGHTNESS

There was this great circle of gold colour stretching out from this person who
was sitting upon the throne and who was so full of light.

I was not able to understand the great circle of gold colour in any way since
it extended from the east to the west and to the south.

The circle did not have any end.

This circle was so high that I could not comprehend it.

This circle shone its *brightness* forth . . . the brightness spread itself out everywhere – upward to the height of heaven and downward to the depth of
the abyss.

> I was not able to see any end to it.
>
> [SCa, p. 177: 3.V1]

☙

(God says:)

All Being is reflected in Myself, who am *Love.* My brilliance reveals the form
of things, just as a shadow indicates a figure.

> [DWe, p. 207: V8.2]

Wisdom is of such kind that no man can conceive of her as she really is; but each strives according to the measure of his wit to understand her if he may;

For Wisdom is of *God*.

King Alfred, 849–901
[inscription found in King Alfred Pub, Saxon Rd, Winchester]

Theme One: Approaching the Creator

INCOMPREHENSIBILITY

Divinity is terrifying yet alluring to every creature,
    seeing and observing all things.

It cannot ever in the depth of God's mystery
    be brought down to the limits
    of human understanding.

                       [SC 3.V9.25, new translation by Brian Pickett]

It is not possible for you to contemplate the divine brightness
    – which cannot be seen by any mortal person –
    unless I show it as in a shadow to whom I will.
Therefore take care that you do not rashly presume
    to cast your eyes on what is divine.
The trembling which seizes you will tell you this.

                       [SC 3.V4.14, new translation by Brian Pickett]

St Bernard of Clairvaux, who lived 1090–1153, was Hildegard's spiritual director from the time she first presented him with an early copy of her *Scivias* in 1147, until his death. His influence and encouragement during these first years of her public life were of enormous importance to her. Although women at that time – and particularly religious women – were expected to be submissive, self-effacing, and totally obedient, Bernard urged Hildegard to unveil her writings and come out into the open with her Visions.

Hildegard's inborn hesitancy combines with her sense of the great awefulness of God and radiates through this extract. Bernard himself wrote ecstatically about the love of God. His own monastic tradition centred on meditation and mystery. William Johnston describes his mystical theology in these terms: 'to go to God one leaves all rationalization and enters into wordless silence, for no-one has ever seen God. Consequently, to circumscribe God, to put God into categories or formulae, to put God into a conceptual framework is to demean God and borders on blasphemy' (*Mystical Theology*, Harper Collins, 1995, p. 45).

As St Paul says, in this life we can only see through a glass darkly (1 Cor. 13:12).

FEARFULNESS

I appear in the fold of my soul as ashes of ashen decay and as a dusty changeableness where I sit, quaking in the shade as a feather.

I labour with great sweat with this vision. Because of the worthlessness of my foolish senses in my flesh, I frequently reckon myself in the least and cheapest place. I am not worthy to be called a person.

I am full of fear, and I do not dare to speak your mystery.

O good and gentle God, teach me what of your will there may be that I ought to say. O you awesome God and most sweet One – so full of every grace – do not forsake me, but keep me in your mercy.

[SCa, p. 178: 9 3.V1]

Teach us, O Lord,
to fear without being afraid;
to fear Thee
that we may love without fear;
through Jesus Christ Our Lord.

[Christina Rossetti, 1830–95]

Many of the classical mystic writers urge us to search for God in a manner that is 'steadfast', but at the same time to be aware of the dangers of spiritual 'greed'. God will disclose to each of us, as unique individuals, what He sees is wise for our growth, but we are not to over-press Him for more. Meister Eckhart, the author of *The Cloud of Unknowing*, Aelred and Madame Guyon are examples of writers who all make the same point as Hildegard. Dame Julian puts it like this:

> It is God's will that we have great regard to all His deeds that He hath done, but evermore it needeth us to leave the beholding what shall be. Then only shall we have joy in God and be well pleased both with hiding and with shewing.
>
> For I saw soothly in Our Lord's meaning, the more we busy ourselves to know His privities, the farther shall we be from the knowing thereof. (ch. 33, p. 59)

> Then ought we to rejoice in Him for all that He sheweth and all that He hideth . . . and therein we shall find great ease. (ch. 36, p. 63)

> And in these words I saw a marvellous high privity hid in God, which privity he shall openly make known to us in Heaven. (ch. 27, p. 49)

> By gracious touch and sweet lighting of the ghostly life we are kept in sure faith, hope, and charity, contrition and devotion, and also with contemplation. (ch. 71, p. 145)

> [*Revelations of Divine Love*, Dom Roger Hudleston (ed.),
> Burns & Oates, London, 1927]

OUR STEADFASTNESS

Blessed steadfastness:

Through piety the church brings forth its miracles, even though it sometimes suffers under the trampling of false words now and then.

[SCa, p. 33: 1.V3.1]

You ought to believe faithfully and not investigate stubbornly *how*: . . . you will not be able to recognise the mysteries of God more than the Holy Spirit wishes to have them revealed to humans.

[SCa, p. 291: 3.V8.8]

God should not be called upon by those who are so mad that they want always to be undisciplined in their knowledge . . . forsaking the well-worn way and well-ploughed field.

[SCa, p. 291: 3.V8.8]

You are turned this way and that by the staggering of your soul . . . Similarly, herbs cannot understand boundaries because they do not know what they are and what their own fruitfulness is for, although they are very useful. And gnats and ants and similar animals do not know or understand the significance of a lion. Likewise, you are not able to know what there may be in the knowledge of God.

[SCa, p. 324: 3.V10.5]

Therefore, work diligently and you will receive fruitfulness. Lift yourself up with dignity and touch the clouds. Many seek me with a devoted, pure, and simple heart; and coming to me, they hold onto me.

[SCa, p. 325: 3.V10.5]

Are Hildegard's ideas about approaching God different to yours? In what way?

Do Hildegard's ideas make God more holy for you, or more difficult?

Would you like to amend her ideas, or do you want to change yours?

How would any such changes affect your own approach to God?

HIS DELIGHT

God the Father had such delight in Himself that He called forth the whole
   creation through His Word.
And then His creation pleased Him too.
And every creature that He lovingly touched, He took in His arms.
O, what great delight you have in your work.

[SCd, p. 52: ch. 8 endnote 8
(from Fuhr-Kotter's translation of Hildegard's Letters)]

　　　　　　　　　　　　　　　　᎑

God loveth that He might *be* Love.
Infinitely delightful to all objects,
Infinitely delighted in all, and
Infinitely pleased in Himself, for being infinitely delightful to all.
All this He attaineth by Love.

[Thomas Traherne, *Centuries*, C2, section 42]

Theme Two:

What God Is Like

Illustration overleaf:
God is growth, rising sap . . . the green-ness of life-giving breath.

GOD IS . . .

The divine majesty . . . with a seeing eye to which all things are naked.

[SCa, p. 32: 3.V1.12]

☙❧

The Omnipotent and Living God

– is incomprehensible, because He cannot be divided by any division or known
  as He is by any part of any of His creatures' knowledge
– in His most glorious serenity was never darkened by any iniquity
– is inextinguishable, because He is that Fullness that no limit ever touched
– is wholly living, for there is nothing that is hidden from Him
– is wholly life, for everything that lives takes its life from Him.

[SCb, p. 150: 2.V1.1]

– *the green-ness of life-giving breath, white with holiness.*

[SCa, p. 136: 2.V6.11]

– sweet moisture, *viriditas.*

[SCa, p. 82: 2.V1.8]

☙❧

God enkindles, sets fire to, and illuminates, all things without changing in
time and finding further goodness; because God is God.

[SCa, p. 183: 3.V1.12]

☙❧

God has not been, but is.

[SCa, p. 182: 3.V1.10]

God was not separated from the Word.

God sent the Word as if the Word were a great fountain from which every
  faithful person could drink so that his or her throat would not be thirsty
  and dry. In this great peacefulness, all who had come earlier admired the
  Word.*

[SCa, p. 84: 2.V1.11]

※

This person (the Word) poured light into the darkness.

The Word . . . sent forth the light-giving blessedness of learning into the
darkness of unfaithfulness . . . and freed . . . the chosen ones who had been
led astray by the devil.

Tambourines and lutes and songs of various musicians were played very
elaborately because the Word . . . was lifted up in blessedness.

The Word went forth, having freed death through heavenly virtues.

[SCa, p. 84–5: 2.V1.13]

THE WORD

The Word is life in burning love.
The Word loosens sins released, with serene brightness.
The Word exists as the very beginning of holiness in a person before that
person can be aroused in holiness.

[SCa, p. 179: 3.V1]

❦

The Word rules powerfully over all who have been touched healthfully by the
Holy Spirit.

[SCa, p. 335: 3.V10.14]

❦

In the Son of God justice and peace were unveiled.
He turned the works of man to better ends,
by destroying the futile,
and conserving the useful.

[DWf, p. 155: LDO V10 ch. 6]

❦

The Word of God came with great silence into the dawn.

[SCa, p. 179: 3.V1]

Hildegard's writings are filled to the brim with countless phrases of God's sayings starting with 'I am . . .'. It would be purposeless to catalogue them, they are recounted so frequently. Among them her favourite images are of God saying:

I AM fire and power
I AM breeze, wind, breath – bringing alive
I AM rain – sustaining, quenching, revivifying, moisturising, greening
I AM love – seeking, attracting, receiving, flowing
I AM delight and gladness – soothing, lifting
I AM reason – giving speculative knowledge – and wisdom
I am aglow – I am afire – I awaken
I AM **life**

[See DWe, pp. 10, 11 and elsewhere]

In the Gospels, Jesus says of himself:

I am the door
I am the bread of life
I am the vine
I am the good shepherd
I am the living water
I am the light of the world
I am the way, the truth, and the life
I am the resurrection and the life
The Father and I are one

GOD SAYS 'I AM...'

I AM life itself.
For I am the whole of life – life was not torn from stones;
it did not bud from branches;
nor is it rooted in the generative power of the male.
Rather, every living thing is rooted in me.

I am of service, since all living things take their radiance from me;
I am the life that remains the same through eternity . . .

Eternity is called the Father,
the Word is called the Son,

and the breath that connects these two is called the Holy Spirit.

[DWe, p. 92: 1,2]

God says:
I AM the breeze that nurtures all things green . . .
I AM the rain coming from the dew that causes the grasses to laugh with joy
of life.
I AM the yearning for good.

[Durka, p. 27 quoting Uhlein, p. 31 DOD 1, 2]

THE ANGELS

Should you hear them singing among stars
or whispering secrets of a wiser world,
do not imagine ardent fledgling children.

They are intelligences old as sunrise
that never learnt right from left, before from after,
knowing but one direction, into God,
    and one duration, now.

Their melody strides not from bar to bar
but like a painting hangs there entire,
one chord of limitless communication.

You have heard it in the rhythms of the hills,
the spiralling turn of a dance, the fall of words
or touch of fingers at the rare, right moment,
    and these were holy, holy.

John V. Taylor, 1992
personal correspondence

WITH ANGELS

I saw heavenly spirits on high in the heavenly mysteries. They were shining very brightly: the looks on their faces appeared as if they were pure water. Resounding with wondrous voices – accompanied with every type of music – they were glorifying God magnificently.

[SCa, p. 67: 1.V6*]

The all-powerful and unutterable God placed certain creatures among earthly things and other creatures among heavenly things ... for the salvation of people and for the honour of God.

[SCa, p. 68: 1.V6.1]

These angelic spirits appeared as if there [sic] were the image of the Word of God shining in a mirror. They stood among those things which the human eye cannot penetrate but which the vision of the inner human can stretch to. The angelic spirits show the beauty of the rationality that is inside themselves. They also pay attention to the will of God in people.

[SCa, p. 69:1.26.2#]

Hildegard had a very distinct and visual idea of God; what images of God are real for you?

Is God 'personal' or 'impersonal'? Distant or close? Would you want this to change?

Sometimes our picture of God can become too chummy. Is intimacy with God incompatible with awe-fulness? Does Hildegard's sense of brightness and burning together *with moisturing*, help with this?

If Hildegard has affected your idea of God at all, how does this relate to your attitude towards those around you?

The brightness of God shines in the good works, so that God can be known, adored, and worshipped lovingly on earth, and that the virtues of people can embellish the holy city with their decorations.

[SCa, p. 342: 3.V10.31]

❧

True faith draws and unites with itself all the virtues, just as wine is poured into a vessel and given to people to drink.

The faithful, exulting and rejoicing in true confidence, carry the bundles of good works they have performed. They taste and drink virtues, and through this they are strengthened, just as the veins of someone drinking are filled with wine. They cannot be satiated in any way, since they always delight in contemplation of the divine.

So the righteous love God, because they find in him no source of weariness, only an enduring blessedness.

[DWc, p. 94: 2, 19,#]

❧

Dame Julian of Norwich says of God: 'Then I saw the Lord royally reign in his own house, fulfilling it with joy and mirth, himself endlessly to gladden and to solace his dearworthy friends, with marvellous melody of endless love' (*Revelations of Divine Love*, ch. 14, Dom Hudleston, ed., Burns Oates, 1927, p. 28).

Theme Three:

Our Response

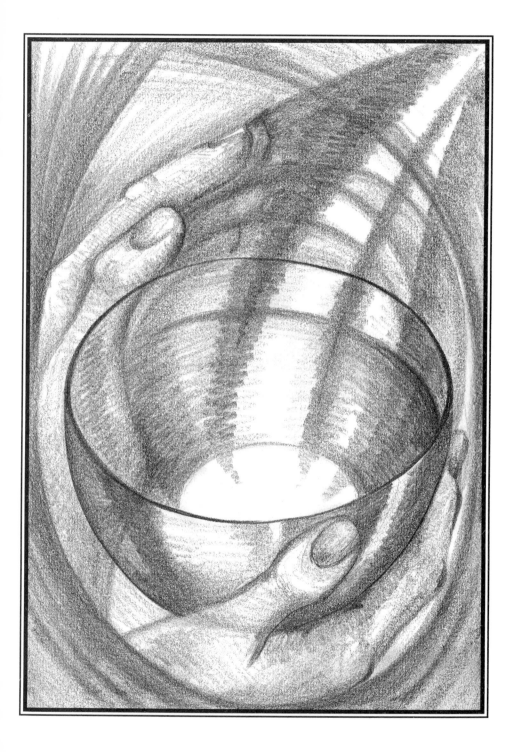

YIELDING TO WETNESS

Yielding ourselves to the Word's brightness and wetness . . .
As dew comes from the clouds and covers the earth with its moisture, so
also good works from God have been moisturised for growing by the
pouring over of the Holy Spirit.

[SCa, p. 29: 1.V3.4]

❦

The soul is saturated with innermost holiness, for people are surrounded
by their Saviour.

[SCa, p. 238: 3.V5.32]

❦

People ought to be nourished from the Cup in order to prevent their
blood from being turned into dryness.

[SCa, p. 150: 2.V6.29]

There is a logical progression in Hildegard's argument that underpins all her work.

1. God is the Shining One.
2. All we have to do is to yield, to receive, to mirror, to become *saturated* by His goodness.
3. Then we can be built up by the *Virtues*,
4. and we become *fruitful*,
5. and *useful*.

But

6. freshness can be lost, and then we become *dry* and *lukewarm*; eventually we shall be burned by the devil and come to be like charcoal.

So

7. it is up to each one of us to *choose ardently* to receive the goodness and moisturising-power that God offers us.

There are strong resonances here with the teaching of Jesus Christ that we are to be like a mustard seed, or a lump of yeast, or some salt, or a lamp – *all of which have to 'receive' before they can be of any 'usefulness'*. Hildegard herself says she is a feather being blown by the breath of God, or a musical instrument being played by God – it is noteworthy that all of these images are primarily 'passive', before they are 'activated' by the power and purpose of God and come to fruitfulness.

FRUITFULNESS

Through the desire for fruitfulness, a person is called to life.

[SCa, p. 229: 3.V5.6]

※

People should retain a glimmering of their knowledge of God.
They should allow God to return to the centre of their lives, recognising that
they owe their very existence to no one else save God alone, who is the
Creator of all.

[LWc, p. 87: LM 4.67]

※

God says:
When I choose, the earth bears so abundantly that people have the fullest
sufficiency, or even more. And so too are people sustained by Me.
To a person who willingly and with good heart receives the seed of My word,
I grant the gifts of the Holy Spirit in superabundance, as to a good field.
One who now receives My word and now refuses to accept it, is like a
field that is sometimes green and sometimes dried up. This person does
not perish utterly: his soul suffers hunger, but he has some greenness,
though not much.

[SCb, p. 475: 3.V10.4]

TWO 'PARABLES' FROM HILDEGARD

A Lord eagerly wishes to build a garden without delay. He fills it with all kinds of plants and then plants good, fruitful trees. Such a garden is full of usefulness, taste, and various good aromas. The same Lord, being a great thinker and profound builder, arranged all the plants according to their goodness and usefulness. He next planted colourful things, watching the moistness of the place, in order that these things may be beautiful.

O people, consider carefully: the Lord plans to destroy his garden if it brings no fruit nor any usefulness.
Why then does such a thinker and builder prepare, plant, water, and protect that garden with such great enthusiasm and with such hard work?

[SCa, p. 22: 1.V2.32*]

Hear therefore! and understand!

God, the Sun of Justice, made His splendour rise over the filth that is man's wickedness. That splendour shone with great brightness, as that filth stank exceedingly. The Sun gleamed forth in its brightness, and the filth putrefied in its foulness. Therefore the Sun was embraced by those beholding it with much greater love than if the filth had not been there opposite it.

Hence justice, being beautiful, must be loved and iniquity, being foul, must be rejected.

[SCb, p. 88: 1.2.32]

USEFULNESS

You were unknowing and unpowerful in giving yourself life . . . but you can move yourself to know the fruit of *usefulness*.

[SCa, p. 321: 3.V10.1]

❧

This is the fact, that a person must first bend his or her hand toward the work, before the hand can do the work.

[SCa, p. 343: 3.V10.32]

❧

The sins which we unsuitably desire . . . lead us to uselessness and evil ways.

[SCa, p. 73, 70: 1.V6.12/4#]

❧

The Holy Spirit supports the happy soul faithfully to complete its good works.

[SCa, p. 53: 1.V4.22]

❧

You were unknowing and unpowerful: but a spirit, together with motion and sensitivity, was given to you so that you can be moved.

[SCa, p. 321: 3.V10.1]

Thy Presence come between me
          and all things evil;
Thy Presence come between me
          and all things vile;
Thy Presence come between me
          and all things of guile;
Thy Presence come between me
          and all things that defile;

Keep me, O Lord, as the apple of Thine eye
Hide me under the shadow of Thy wings.

David Adam, *The Edge of Glory*, prayers in the Celtic tradition,
Triangle SPCK, London, 1985

CARELESSNESS AND WEARINESS

When a person loses the freshness of God's power, he is transformed into the
    dryness of carelessness.
He lacks the juice and greenness of good works and the energies of his heart
    are sapped away.

                         [Letter to a cleric, quoted SCd, p. 64, DOD, p. 70]

You are lukewarm and wither into yourselves disgracefully, because you do
    not want to open up even one eye to see what you can do in the goodness
    of your spirit.

                                  [SCa, p. 321: 3.V10.1]

Time will bring forth people who are playful in the flood of sin,
    the blackness of sadness,
    the mud of uncleanness,
    and with the weariness of feebleness . . .
They leap across the performance of good virtues with the quickness of their
    own pleasures.
They will have contrariness.

                                [SCa, p. 347: 3.V10.4*]

These fleeting times will vanish.
For people rise and set like the sun, and some are born, and some die.

                                    [SCb, p. 495: 3.V11.6]

In the days of Hildegard, there was little stimulation for her nuns that was allowed in from outside of the convent. There is small wonder that she exhorted them to beware of sluggishness; at times the monotony must have seemed unbearable. Hildegard herself was enormously creative, and the whole community would have been affected by the music she composed for them, the singing she nurtured among them, the artistry of her dictated illuminations, and the healing activity of her herbal remedies. Nonetheless, she was away from the convent travelling a great deal, and in her writings she is constantly aware of the dangers of middle-of-the-road boredom and lukewarmness.

In contrast, today we live in an avalanche of perpetual stimulation. Super-energised voices from broadcasters, high-pitched advertising claims, loud and large headlines, internet surfing, all compete for our attention: the sources of arousal are formidable.

As a result of being constantly over-charged, do we become under-reactive? If we are mentally and emotionally saturated, we tend to shut off, and become dulled. Almost as dull as if we were under-stimulated?

In your own response to God, there may be times when you feel lackadaisical towards him; is this on account of too little challenge or too much?

Do you catch yourself being unwilling to make yet another effort in getting to know God better?

Are you going to do anything about it? Are you going to try once more, and try even harder?

Or can you take time out just to receive; to absorb; to wonder; to be enfolded, and clothed?

BEWARE LUKEWARMNESS

It is not possible to enter the divine brightness,
but beware lukewarmness.

[SCa, p. 215: 3.V4.14]

Very often people are weak in their hearts, and insultingly sleepy in their
actions.
Being at leisure, they stay away from the wondrous works of blessedness . . .
in the lukewarmness of their crookedness.

[SCa, p. 10: 1.V1.5/6]

Being inactive, she knew the law of God which she received by divine consideration externally; but she did not know it inwardly, under the weariness
of her sluggishness.

[SCa, p. 61: 1.V5.5]

There are people being taught who are lukewarm and dull; therefore extend
yourself in the fountain of abundance, so that those who wish may be
aroused by the flowing of your water.

[SCa, p. 7: 1.V6]

Drink with hope this wine; . . .
as a result, you will be *intoxicated with charity.*

[SCa, p. 143: 2.V6.21]

Theme Four:

Zeal

Illustration overleaf:
Every creature yearns to stretch itself in its search for God,
and yearns for a loving embrace.
I lift the broken-hearted and lead them to wholeness.
I am balm for every pain.

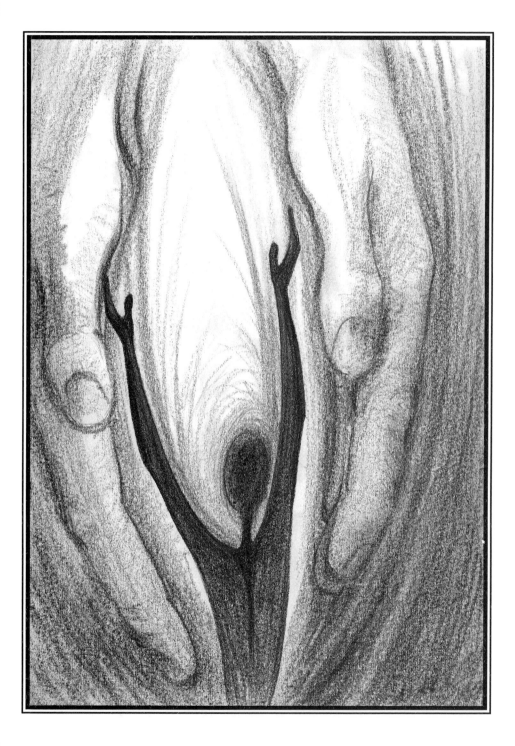

THE ZEAL OF GOD

In God, *zeal* is most swift and sharp
    to kill the devil and all evil.
God, who worked hard and grievously with zeal among the people of old,
    has been shown to be gentle and delightful with the new people for love
    of the Son.

[SC, 3.V5.1, Brian Pickett, new translation]

The somewhat longer extract on the opposite page includes several ideas that are very typical of Hildegard's teaching. They go something like this:

1. It is natural and proper that we yearn to stretch ourselves to our fullest extent as we search for God.
2. But we can only go so far towards Him and no further. His zeal for us is inexhaustible; ours for Him is inevitably limited.
3. Our zeal for Him has to have its boundaries: He has no boundaries and complete understanding of Him by us is unreachable. We approach His infinitude in our finiteness. Our search has to be grounded and restrained by our enfleshment.
4. The bodies which were created by God and put into our care are to be treasured by us, but they must also be held with a certain sense of distrust. Too much reliance on them and their fleshly appetites can lead us away from God.
5. If we are prepared to acknowledge this ambivalence, then when we lapse from being 'moistened' by God, our soul will come to our rescue.

OUR ZEAL MUST BE LIMITED

The soul ascends to the heights, where it experiences God.

No matter how eager the soul may be to do as much good as possible within the body, it cannot go further than divine grace permits it to go.

The soul rejoices at being able to achieve things with the body.

The soul cannot achieve more than the limits of our bodily elements allow.

That body has been formed by God, and thus the soul is most anxious to perfect the body's work.

The soul itself experiences the functions of the entire body: thus the soul can ascend into the brain, the heart, the blood or the marrow.

Often the soul does things according to the desires of the flesh, until the blood dries out more and more in our veins as a result of exhaustion, and until sweat is ejected through our marrow. At this point, the soul will retreat into inactivity until it can again warm up the blood of the flesh and replenish the marrow.

The soul urges the body to be vigilant and revives it to do its proper work.

It will turn again totally to do God's service, and it will rise up to God and say 'Hide me in the silence of your very great power. For I remain under the power of the wicked even though I beseech you, revere you, and place no trust in an alien or false God'.

Thus the soul says: 'O my flesh and my limbs, in which I have my dwelling, how much do I rejoice that I have been sent to you who are in agreement with me.'

[DWe, p. 95–6: 4.19*]

Zeal for goodness is like a day when we can ponder everything in our mind, while laziness is like a night when we can no longer see anything at all. Just as the night is often moonlit and then later overshadowed, our deeds are all mixed up. It often happens that our flesh may feel bored when it co-operates with the soul. The soul may give in to its fleshly partner and let the flesh take delight in earthly things. Similarly, a mother knows how to get her crying child to laugh again.

Thus the soul accomplished good deeds with the body, even though there may be some evil mixed up with them.

[DWe, p. 101: V4.24*]

François Malaval, 1627–1719, echoes something of Hildegard. She says:

> I have attempted to take you into the garden of the Bridegroom, but not to describe to you the fruits and flowers. This garden is vast and great; it is for Him to lead you along its paths as it pleases Him. Be faithful to God, and God will be liberal to you.
>
> Never try to go before God; follow Him always, and do not trouble about anything but loving Him, never mind if you cannot see Him.

A Simple Method of Raising the Soul,
Second Treatise, Dialogue XII

Madam Guyon, 1648–1717, also wrote in a similar way:

> It is thus with souls.
> (i) Some go on quietly towards perfection, and never reach the sea – or only very late – contented to lose themselves in some stronger river which carries them with itself into the sea.
> (ii) Others flow on more vigorously and promptly than the first. They even carry with them a number of rivulets. But in comparison to the last class they are slow and idle.
> (iii) The last class rush onward with so much impetuosity that they are utterly useless: they are not available for navigation, nor can any merchandise be trusted upon them. These are bold and mad rivers, which dash against the rocks, which terrify by their noise, and which stop at nothing.
>
> The second class are more agreeable and more useful: their gravity is pleasing, they are all laden with merchandise, and we sail upon them without fear or peril.

Spiritual Torrents, Part I, Ch. I

Both these extracts are quoted in
A Dazzling Darkness, Patrick Grant (ed.),
Fount, London, 1985, pp. 171, 173.

O HAPPY SOUL!

Your body has risen from the earth,
    which You trod in your journeying of this world.
Made to be the mirror of God,
    You have been crowned with Divine reasoning.

And the Holy Spirit has looked upon You
    as God's own dwelling place.
Made to be the mirror of God,
    You have been crowned with Divine reasoning.

Glory to the Father, and to the Son,
    and to the Holy Spirit.

[*O Felix Anima*, SACR 64, Brian Pickett, new translation]

It is a crucially humbling notion, that God is more zealous for me than I am for Him. That He is more concerned with the life I could live with Him than I am myself. Shall I really take such an idea on board, or shall I just leave it with Hildegard?

Hildegard's descriptions of the interaction between soul and body were written eight centuries before the more general understanding we now enjoy. They are expressed in language that is unfamiliar, and some of the specific details are awkward to our ears: what words would you use to illustrate the relationship between God, our souls and our bodies?

When I feel enthusiastic and zealous for God, how much do I take that for my own merit? Is my keenness a means of polishing my own halo?

Are there occasions when my own zealousness is in fact an ego-boosting exercise, and it makes others simply shut off? Do I need sometimes to curb my enthusiasm in order to allow God to work directly with others, instead of through me? Such as . . .?

HARDNESS OF HEART

Hardness of heart says:

Why should I bother about anything?

God created everything, let Him take care of it all.

If I became involved, even just a little, what use would it do me? And even if
I did, I could go around feeling pity for everyone and everything, but I
wouldn't get a moment's peace; and what would become of me? What
kind of life would I lead if I had to find an answer for every voice of joy
or sadness?

I know only that I myself exist, and everyone else should do the same.

Mercy's reply:

Every creature yearns for a loving embrace.

The plants give off the fragrance of their flowers.

The precious stones reflect their brilliance to others.

All you are is a pitiless stare.

I am a soothing herb. I dwell in the dew and in the air and in all greenness.
My heart fills to overflowing and I give help to others. I was there when
the first words resounded: '*Let there be*'.

With a loving eye, I observe the demands of life and feel myself part of it all.
I lift the broken-hearted and lead them to wholeness.

I am balm for every pain, and my words ring true.

[LWc, pp. 85–6: 1.16–17*]

Theme Five:

Day by Day

Illustration overleaf:
*Knowing two footpaths, by their innermost choice
they embrace God with complete desire.*

ARDENTLY CHOOSING

Offer
the struggles
of the questions,
which result in personal wars and tumults;
for
when
the question is not in a person,
then
neither is the answer of the Holy Spirit.

[SCa, p. 70: 1.V6.4]

As long as this question and answer are in a person, the power of God will not be absent; for this question and answer carries with it penitence.

[SCb, p. 141: 1.V6.4]

Ardently choose God and embrace God with complete desire . . .

[SCa, p. 73: 1.V6.10]

People watch and know two footpaths, clearly good and evil; people should be moved by one of these two.
Their choice is made in their soul.

[SCa, p. 192: 3.V2.4]

People can love God by their own innermost choice and can offer devotion to God.

[SCa, p. 217: 3.V4.15]

That is certainly to avoid evil with the keenest consideration, and to choose good.

[SCa, p. 192: 3.V2.4]

From *The Independent Review*, Sunday 22 January 1985

On *boredom*: The English had previously used the French word 'ennui' to describe a mood of spiritual languor, but there was a need for something less metaphysically dignified.

When people began to ease free from the realm of public conduct and foster their private sensibilities, boredom was their first reward. Boredom belongs to the age of secular identity and the creation of leisure time.

To compensate for this ever-growing void in the inner life, there was a rush of distractions from the outside world, all testifying to the fear of running out of things to do. There was a 200-year weakening of attention . . . a world gradually giving way to the thirst for distraction.

When moral quandaries begin to fade and there is this thirst for distraction, the loosening of ethical life approaches terminal entropy.

Then boredom and the trivial have experienced their greatest flowering.

Matt Ffytche

Is there a connection between too much astonishment, and boredom born of saturation?

What happens then?

RUSHING WITH ASTONISHMENT

The devil uses astonishment to rush people along, so they will follow him. They cover over their inner eyes.

[SCa, pp. 357, 355: 3.V11.30/27]

You are turned this way and that by the staggering of your soul.

[SCa, pp. 324: 3.V10.5]

※

The devil . . . sends out craftiness and confusion in every direction; he spreads wickedness and worthlessness with blowing and with scattering.

[SCa, p. 308: 3.V9.2]

A life all turbulent may seem –
To him that leads it – wise,
And to be praised . . .

But Wisdom is a pearl with most success
Sought in still waters.

William Cowper, *The Task*, Book III

RUNNING TO AND FRO

There was an open market square where the riches of people and various worldly delights appeared. In the square people were running swiftly, but doing no business.

[SCa, p. 161: 2.V7]

Some people want to joke and play around with me: they want to approach me without the work of their soul. They want to seize me as if they just woke up from a deep sleep, seizing the way of holiness unexpectedly with the pretense and deception they often contrive within themselves.

[SCa, p. 325: 3.V10.6]

Your spirit is pressed down by the restlessness of your foolish soul.

[SCa, p. 324:3.V10.5]

The power of the Trinity punishes the people who run to and fro in various ways.

[SCa, p. 234. 3.V5.14]

So it is

that all of us who have been redeemed through the Son of God

will **exult** with our whole body

and **rejoice** with our whole soul

in you,

O Holy Godhead.

[SCc, p. 93: DW2.19*]

SEXUAL LOVE

There will be and there must be one and the same love in man and in woman.

The man's love, compared with the woman's, is a heat of ardour like a fire on blazing mountains, which can hardly be put out; whilst hers is a wood-fire that is easily quenched.

But the woman's love, compared with the man's, is like a sweet warmth proceeding from the sun, which brings forth fruits.

Because a man feels this great sweetness in himself, and is like a stag thirsting for the fountain, he races swiftly to the woman and she to him – she like a threshing floor pounded by his many strokes and brought to heat when the grains are threshed inside her.

[SCc, p. 108: Dronke 176, 244; Kaiser 136–7]

☸

The soul has an understanding of what the body demands since the body really derives its life from the soul.

[DWe, p. 93: V4.17]

Where would one find people who could refuse to carry out the desires of the flesh – even if they wished to!

For we can judge the good, and have the pure gift of decision making.

If we exceed our proper dimension in what is good, we may fall down into the abyss, and we will be completely ruined in despair.

But –

Even if our repentance were to rise up over all the deserts and all the waters of the sea, we could hardly realize what salvation means with all its joys of eternal life and indescribable rapture.

These are the tasks by which the soul lives in the body and achieves much within it in accordance with the requirements of the body.

And therefore we humans are steeped in goodness.†

[DWe, pp. 108, 109*: V:IV, 33/34]

---

† Hildegard adds, ' . . . goodness by day, and evil by night'!

MENSTRUATION AND THE FOUR TEMPERAMENTS OF WOMAN

1. (*De sanguinea*) Some women have soft and delectable flesh; and in love's embraces are themselves lovable. At menstruation they suffer only a moderate loss of blood, and their womb is well developed for childbearing, so they are fertile and can take in the man's seed.

2. (*De flecmatica*) These women have a somewhat mannish disposition. At menstruation their menstrual blood flows neither too little nor too abundantly. Because they have thick veins they are very fertile and conceive easily, for their womb and all their inner organs, too, are well developed. They attract men and make men pursue them, and so men love them well. If they want to stay away from men, they can do so without being affected by it badly, though they are slightly affected.

3. (*De colerica*) They suffer much loss of blood in menstruation, their womb is well developed and they are fertile. Men flee from them and avoid them ... for they can interest men but not make men desire them. If they do get married, they are chaste, loyal, and live healthily with their husbands.

4. (*De melancolica*) They are changeable and free-roaming in their thoughts, and wearisomely wasted away in affliction. They suffer much loss of blood in menstruation and they are sterile, because they have a weak and fragile womb. They cannot lodge or retain or warm a man's seed. Thus they are healthier, stronger and happier without husbands – especially because, if they lie with their husbands, they will tend to feel weak afterwards. Yet some such women, if they unite with robust and sanguine husbands, can, at times, when they reach a fair age, such as fifty, bear at least one child. . . . if they are not helped in their illness (melancholia) so that they are freed from it either by God's help or by medicine, they will quickly die.

[SCc, pp. 108, 110*: Dronke 180–1, 247–9; Kaiser 879]

Many of the ideas expressed by Hildegard which connect bodiliness and sin are unfamiliar to our ears today. Their eleventh-century culture bears a heavy emphasis on the highest virtue of all, which is virginity. When they are extracted from the accompanying fervour, they do contain an astonishing degree of good sense.

1. In what ways do I 'plunder my body'?

2. If indeed I can 'judge the good', how often do I betray this judgement? And how often do I support it?

3. Do I exult and rejoice with my soul and my body *together*?

4. Can I recognise distractions for what they are, or do I take them for real?

5. So when do I 'ardently choose'? To what end?

PLUNDERING OURSELVES

People embrace bitterness in contradiction to good.

They *plunder* themselves by carrying the good treasures (the Virtues) away from themselves.

They cross themselves up with the boldness of their own wishes, not wishing to restrain their bodies.

Such people are unwashed and withered.

[SCa, p. 230: 3.V5.7]

Those who think they were born to be unhappy

As soon as some people find themselves faced with the vicissitudes of everyday life, they start to mistrust God. They decide that they must be fated to be unhappy.

'God does not want to help us' they claim, 'and He can't do so either. We are stuck with the life of misery.'

Human beings are by nature good. It is their own fault if they pervert their true natures and give rein to their arbitrary desires.

Let the faithful take care to keep this firmly fixed in the memory of their good conscience.

[LWc, p. 86: LM2.93]

Theme Six:

The Opposer – Lucifer

Illustration overleaf:
Poisonous madness . . . bristling, breaking, striking, sins.

THE EXALTATION OF EVIL

Mortal people are not strong enough to understand all of the poisonous madness and deceitfulness of the devil.

[SCa, p. 164: 2.V7.3]

∿

No person is able to know the exaltation of the evil in the entrails of the devil.

[SCa, p. 201: 3.V2.28]

∿

The persuasiveness of the devil tames some people with its evilness and bends them to its faults; this leads to the *taming of our good intentions*, so we cannot comprehend the profoundness of the issues of good and evil.

[SCa, p. 171: 2.V7.15#]

∿

Bristling,
   breaking,
      striking,
         sins.

[SCa, p. 283: 2.V1.8]

The vivid visual images which attack Hildegard in her visions are experienced by her through the senses, as much as through the mind and imagination. For her, these effects are reality.

Have we, in our sophistication, distanced ourselves from them too far? The indignity of the devil and all his activities enrage Hildegard. She flares out at him in powerful language, using horrendous images: there is nothing 'quaint' about the fury she levels at him. She says:

Lucifer is a hideous blackness;

he is
- flaming
- a writhing, stinging worm of unimaginable horribleness
    with bloodshot, fiery eyes
    round and hairy ears
    full of sores and pus
- there are very sharp arrows coming from the mouth of the worm
    depicting the worst rage
- black smoke rushes from its breast
    depicting the worst of anger and envy
- flaming fluid is boiling up from its loins
    depicting the boiling desires, the uncleanness of the devil
- a whirlwind blows from its navel
    which depicts those who fornicate, choking on their gluttony
- there is a turmoil gushing from the extremity of its belly –
    the stinking waste of despair of those who have followed the devil
- a very foul fog came from this worm:
    it stunk, it infected people with its perversity.

All of these things made a very great disturbance among the people, causing them not to believe in God.

[SCa, p. 173: 2.V7.19/20]

ATTRIBUTES OF THE DEVIL

To Hildegard, Lucifer is a very real and concrete being. He has his own history and biography, his own physical description and idiosyncracies, his own staff and army. Together, they add up to confusion and terror.

Attributes of the devil in Hildegard's writings include:

* false glory . . . leading to bitterness and anxiety in people
* stinging withdrawal . . . leading to misery of heart in people
* worldly sorrow and despondency . . . leading to weakness in both spiritual and worldly things among people
* tasteless irreverence . . . leading to ugliness in people
* lukewarm imitation of God . . . leading to speaking with double tongues among spirits and people

※

People are weakened by the lukewarm taste of evil rumour.

[SCa, p. 7:1.V1]

※

Truth is contrary and irksome to the Devil.

[SCa, p. 243: 3.V6]

※

The Virtues, however, weaken the harsh sourness of the blemishes of the snares of the devil.

[SCa, p. 392: 3.v13.12#]

The Spirit needs us to recognise our true centre
the actual living core of our persons
the unshakeably *real self*;

experiencing what we already possess
deepening what we already have

Our task is to become *who we really are*
to recognise and to reconcile the warring parts within us.

I would dare to suggest that while we fail to recognise the different parts of ourselves on the inside,

we may project them on to others on the outside,

with resulting divisions and barricading and conflict as an external process.

Perhaps not until we have waited on the Lord and with His grace have allowed reconciliation within, can we hope for reconciliation without.

Martin Smith, *A Season for the Spirit*, Fount, London 1991

CRAFTY PERSUASIVENESS

Lucifer offers his wares *so gently* that people are deceived.
With his craftiness he pierces them with blemishes . . .

[SCa, p. 392: 3.V13.13]

. . . or with a boiling whirlwind which results in confusion and foolishness.

[SCa, p. 173: 2.V7.21]

They send away their inner sight and hearing, since they cultivate the devil.

[SCa, p. 356: 3.V11.29]

He proposes to them that they can choose their own God, whom he pretends
to be himself.

[SCa: 3.V11.30]

※

O Lord! Seek us, find us
in Thy patient care

Lest the god of this world blind us
lest he bait a snare.

Lest he forge a chain to bind us
lest he speak us fair.

Turn not from us, call to mind us,
find, embrace, and hear;

Be Thy love before, behind us,
round us, everywhere.

Christina Rossetti 1830–94

What impact does the extract opposite have on you, *now*, as you see it?

How does this Theme of extracts compare with ideas around us today?

Have they affected your attitude or behaviour – is there *one* change you would like to make?

What is it? Would you like to write it down here?

The Devil
still tries
to accomplish more than the Devil can;
although he knows his power is small
since the
incarnation
of the Word
of God

[SCa, p. 167: 2.V7.10]

Theme Seven:

His Fate

Illustration overleaf:
But the devil fell.

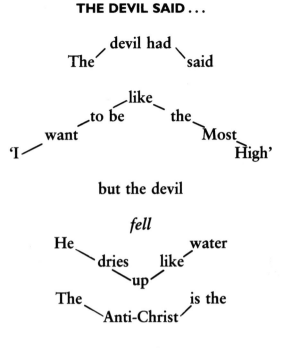

The devil had said

'I want to be like the Most High'

but the devil

fell

He dries up like water

The Anti-Christ is the

worst

beast

[SCa, p. 354: 3.V11.26/27#]

They turned away from God's friendship
with their own blazing pride.

As they did,
all of them were extinguished
and turned into the blackness of burnt wood,

as they gulped down unholiness.

[SCa, p. 185: 3.V1.14]

WHEN LUCIFER REBELLED

The very great multitude of heavenly spirits were created by God, and did not grasp for heavenly glory, but they stood firm in divine love. So that those who reflected the burning brightness took on a most serene brilliance.

But

When Lucifer decided to rebel against the heavenly Creator with (some of) the other angels, they put on the zeal of God as they fell from the Divinity in disagreement. They embraced the dullness of ignorance by which they were not able to know God.

God remained unchanged in power; God was able to conquer without even using a warrior. All those who glowed in God's love despised the dust of injustice.

But Lucifer at first stood special and great because Lucifer did not yet know of Lucifer's weakness in grace and strength. Indeed, when Lucifer thought about grace and the power of self-strength, Lucifer became proud. This caused Lucifer to expect that Lucifer might attempt whatever Lucifer wished, because Lucifer had previously been able to finish whatever Lucifer started.

Lucifer wanted to divide up the wholeness of the divinity.

And when Lucifer was puffed up with pride and wanted to do what Lucifer had just thought about, the zeal of God – extending itself – threw Lucifer (with all his spirits) into the burning blackness. They seethed against the brightness and clearness which they had had, and they were blackened.

The filth of the wanton worthlessness is blazing in the will of those who do not fear God, but who scorn the divinity with perverse madness.

They despise thinking that someone might be strong enough to overcome them when in the fire of their own ignorance they want to burn up what they disturb.

This will happen when they are burning to possess what God does not want them to have. And they will not receive the coming rainfall of the Holy Spirit.

At the time of the final judgement, the despair that all things are vile will come to those who are disloyal to God; tormented sorrow brought on by the rage of their own madness.

[SCa, pp. 13, 15: 1.V2.2–4*#]

As a result, all the elements of the world which previously stood still in a great quietness, were made to display horrible fears and turn into a very great restlessness.

[SCa, p. 13: 1.V2.2]

Hildegard's work is packed solid with descriptions of the goodness of God, of His Brightness and Mercy, His Love and Compassion.

But Hildegard has little patience with those 'who know the highest good and despise it'.

These days we are encouraged to understand the traps and compulsions, the deprivations and conditioning circumstances that colour our decisions and mould our behaviour. We are trained – against our own natures – to be at all costs non-judgemental; we seldom hear the hellfire exhortations that drew hundreds to their knees in the last century.

Have we gone too far? Is it in the interests of the highest good to erase, in the consciousness of people in the high street, a sense of the *power* of evil? Do visual images help as a sort of portable shorthand, in being aware of the alternative to 'seeking the highest good'?

Our headlines, and the way we absorb the daily news using sound-bytes, make suspicion and fear and guarding a common way of life. Our behaviour towards each other feeds on self-defence. What about the concept of being on our guard against evil principalities, rather than evil people?

How would we view our own behaviour, and our own responses then?

At the very least, these are questions that need solemn consideration.

THE LOWER WORLD

The lower world contains the width of imperfections and the depth of ruins.

It sends forth burning smoke with a great stink.

At the same time as it held out pleasantness and sweetness to the souls immersed in it, it perversely deceived these souls and led them to torment where flames arise, giving off the foulest of smoke and a deadly stench.

These frightening tortures were prepared for the devil and the devil's followers because they turned away from the highest good and they did not want either to know or to understand that good.

Therefore they have been cast out from all good – not because they did not know the highest good, but because with their great pride they despised it.

[SCa, pp. 15, 16: 1.V2.5]

All our sins are no match for the inexhaustible initiative of God.

All our sins are no match for the inexhaustible initiative of God.

All our sins are no match for the inexhaustible initiative of God.

All our sins are no match for the inexhaustible initiative of God.

All our sins are no match for the inexhaustible initiative of God.

All our sins are no match for the inexhaustible initiative of God.

All our sins are no match for the inexhaustible initiative of God.

All our sins are no match for the inexhaustible initiative of God.

All our sins are no match for the inexhaustible initiative of God.
Austin Farrer

HE IS NO MATCH FOR GOD

As mud is foul in comparison to the sun, so also
The transgression of humans is unequal to the justice of God.

[SCa, p. 22: 1.V2.32]

God chases away the wrinkled enemy, tearing the chosen ones away from
the jaws of the devil.

[SCa, p. 235: 3.V5.15]

Through the desire of fruitfulness, a person is called to life.

[SCa, p. 229: 3.V5.6]

ॐ

The power of God flies everywhere and surrounds all things, with nothing
resisting it.
The rationality of people holds great strength for listening to the sounds of
the living voice.
And the soul of people can be aroused from sluggishness to watchfulness.

[SCa, p. 391: 3.V13.13*]

Theme Eight:

Our Part in this Drama

Illustration overleaf:
Look inward into yourself.
Look with your inner eye and see the fiery presence of the Spirit.

RATIONALITY AND CHOICE

You are given a gift of profound knowledge, and so have in yourself all you need. This being so, My eyes will search you closely and remember what they find.

[SCb, p. 474: 3.V10.3]

Humans have speculative wisdom and the power of choice.

[SCa, p. 226: 3.V5.1]

※

The Holy Spirit makes the senses and minds of people bright
so that they can understand most keenly all their own motives
and what they should do that is acceptable to God.

[SCa, p. 257: 3.V6.34]

※

Human beings fly with two wings; the right wing is the knowledge of good and the left wing is the knowledge of evil. The knowledge of evil *serves the good* insofar as the good is sharpened and highlighted through the knowledge of evil; and so through this knowledge human beings become wise in all things.

[DWe, p. 350: a letter from Hildegard to Wibert]

Humans ought to work strongly with all their powers of reason joined to the goodness of God;
they ought to work against the devil with a knowledge of good and evil.

[SCa, p. 226: 3.V5.1]

Is the pursuit of self-knowledge 'selfish'? Hildegard is very keen on 'good works', but equally – which is perhaps more surprising for her time – on the *self-knowing* that should precede good works.

People can get carried away by the visible merits of their good works, and use them to boost their own self-image; Hildegard insists that we have to know what drives our intention to do good works, whether it is for the true glory of God, or, just perhaps, the glorification of Me.

Well before the time of Freud and Jung and self-analysis, there were spiritual masters who advocated the idea that self-knowledge came *before* the knowledge of others or, even, the knowledge of God. Some mystical writers contemporary to Hildegard went further and suggested that knowledge of God was not possible without a degree of knowledge of self.

For instance, Hildegard's own spiritual adviser, Bernard of Clairvaux (1090–1153) wrote:

> Therefore, let us know ourselves that we may fear God,
> and let us know God that we may also love him.
> It is as necessary to avoid ignorance of God and ignorance of self as it is
> certain that without the fear and love of God we cannot save our souls.

He rather unfashionably adds:

> As for the knowledge of other objects, that is a matter of indifference; we shall
> not be condemned for the want of it any more than its possession will save us.
> *Sermons*, XXXVII

Another exact contemporary of Hildegard, Hugh of St Victor (1096–1141), wrote:

> Your eye sees nothing well, if it sees not itself.
> If perchance your inner vision is dimmed by neglect, and you have no power to
> contemplate yourself as is fit and profitable, why do you not at least use
> another's judgement to consider what you should think about yourself?
> *The Soul's Betrothal Gift*, p. 10

Three centuries later, classic spiritual writers continue with the same theme: 'It belongeth properly to us, to long and desire with all our mights to know our Self' (ch. 46) and 'we may never come to full knowing of God till we know first clearly our own Soul' (Dame Julian, *Revelations of Divine Love*).

> *Swink and sweat in all thou canst and mayest to get thee a true knowing of*
> *thyself:*
> *then, I trow, thou wilt get thee a true knowing of God, as He is.*
> *Cloud of Unknowing*, Anon

SELF-KNOWING

So, O Person, look inward into yourself.

[SCa, p. 330: 3.V10.8]

☙❧

God says:
They should look at me with their inner eyes . . .

[SCa, p. 355: 3.V11.27]

. . . and find those things which the human eye cannot penetrate, but which the inner eye can stretch to.

[SCa, p. 68: 1.V6.1]

☙❧

All the Virtues threw off the tests of legal institutions,
and their cloaks of earthly cares (i.e. their roles and responsibilities),
and instead
they looked inside themselves for true justice.

[SCa, p. 250: 3.V6.27]

☙❧

God says:
You should have thought about yourself before you called upon me.

[SCa, p. 326: 3.V10.6]

Earlier pages in this book have illustrated Hildegard's sense of evil in 'staggering', 'scattering', 'running to and fro'; here she emphasises her great belief in *constancy.* Another early saint renowned for constancy was:

ST SWITHUN AD 800–62

St Swithun is a most remarkable saint.
As a man, he was not renowned for miracles,
or visions,
or martyrdom,
or mission,
or even inordinate suffering,
(he doesn't appear to have been inordinate about anything).
Nevertheless, he was so loved and remembered that he is the *only* one for whom sainthood was clamoured for by the people.

Three centuries after he died – in the century of Hildegard – there was an uproar concerning how he should be recorded (little had been written down describing him in his lifetime); not only was he then canonised, but his name was added to St Paul and St Peter in the attribution of the cathedral he originally planned.

His distinction was that he was associated with . . . the *Weather*!!!

'Weather' or '*Whether*'?

Swithun's reputation for goodness and blessedness remained constant whether

he was influencing the city (the mayor and corporation)	–	or the Church; (the abbot and his abbey)
he was building bridges (over the town river)	–	or a cathedral; (Winchester's first cathedral)
he was attending to market women (replacing their broken eggs, whole)	–	or the king's son; (tutoring Ethelwolf)
his body lay outside and exposed (to the tramp of feet and bad weather)	–	or inside and venerated; (as a popular pilgrimage site)
whether he was advising kings or priests (King Arthur or cathedral canons)	–	or people of the town

Swithun's reputation of concern and care, and most of all as a *desiderati* (one who desires Christ with utmost longing and searching) was independent of the weather, whether as an ordinary mortal he liked it or not.

His search and his care were uncontained by walls or status or weather. He loved and advised and educated and planned and built and worked for all, and is remembered and loved and emulated for it to this day.

In all the swings and roundabouts, the upturns and downturns, the varieties and diversities and spirals of life, *constancy* is Hildegard's high priority.

CONSIDERATION AND CONSTANCY

God says
They do not consider whether I am salty or not salty,
  sweet or bitter,
  a dweller of heaven or of earth.
They do not pay attention to either the spice or the sweetness of the
  Scriptures; . . . as a result they are strangers to me and are called *fugitives*.

[SCa, p. 118, 119: 2.V5.41]

⚭

They do not want to consider who they are or
  what they are or
  what they are able to accomplish.
They do not want to think, but rather they want to approach me without the
  work of their soul.
They want to joke and play around with me.

[SCa, p. 325: 3.V10.6*#]

⚭

Constancy says:
I am a very strong pillar.
I am not mobile and fickle with instability.
I am not stirred by the wind and flung hither and thither.
I endure by standing on true stone – the true Word of God.

I do not want to be among those who cry because they have been scattered;
they never remain at rest and are not stable.
They are always falling to lower places.
I have been founded upon the strongest of foundations.
I persevere in the true God who will not be stirred for all eternity.

[SCA, p. 333: 3.V10.10*#]

Overheard: "Course I go to church; I pray to God to see what I can get out of 'im.' This is basic, unclouded honesty. This person knows himself. Am I as honest with myself, and as clear about my intentions?

When I know myself sufficiently, and my curtains of self-delusion are drawn back, what do I find?

Do I find myself testing God, using Him for my own ends?

The people in the Gospels who were *against* Christ asked him for a sign:
'Who struck you that time?' asked the soldiers who blindfolded him.
'Give us a sign,' commanded those who tested him.
'Come down from the cross, if indeed you are the Son of God,' they taunted him.
Do I really, never, catch myself doing just this?

How much, in reality, do I rabbit around, investigating 'new' ideas, just for the fun of it? Novelty is a great motivator in our present culture; do I succumb to the excitement of constantly changing my mind about the things of God? Do I want God as my house servant, to do *my* will?

When I pray, do I tell Him what *I* want Him to do?

USING GOD

Others,
Thinking it possible to have everything,
want to have God
as their own
houseservant

who may accomplish their every wish

[SCa, p. 325: 3.v10.6]

Theme Nine:

Hazards and Trials

Illustration overleaf:
I want to communicate with you and be united to your sorrows.
Supporting you, I will save you. . . . I sustain you silently.

THE SELF-TRUST OF LUCIFER

God says:
Lucifer, leaning towards evil, did not look at me, the complete one, but he had complete self-trust ... twisting honour back to himself.

[SCa, p. 184: 3.V1.14]

Lucifer, created shining with brightness, was not able to handle it correctly; he tried to be like God.

[SCa, p. 186: 3.V1.16]

The devil was too self-trusting.

[SCa, p. 119: 2.V5.43]

Whoever prepares a tower for himself (or herself) according to their own will, also despises me.

[SCa, p. 395: 3.V13.16]

A person cannot seize a mountain, and will (on their own) to move it: clearly this is planned only by the kind of person who fans himself into confusion, and who cuts up a piece of fruit without eating it.

[SCa, p. 394: 3.V13.16]

Hildegard highlights a very important, under-considered and fuzzy boundary between proper self-knowing – which she advocates, as we have seen on previous pages – and self-*trust*.

She would say that for me to get to know my own personal strengths and limitations, my preferences and compulsions, and my gifts and flaws is 'useful'. But then to rely solely on my own strength, my own insight, and my own capacity, without reference to the will and power of God, is to mirror the way Lucifer functions.

Is this difference as crucially important as Hildegard says it is?

If it is, where does self-esteem fit in?

Jesus Christ said:
'*Keep awake*:
   Be on your guard:
      keep alert.'

(Luke 21:36)

Is it possible to love myself because God loves me, but also to distrust myself when I cease to be dependent upon Him?

TRUST IN OURSELVES

Those who trust in themselves
rather than in Me
Despise having trust in Me
Counting the grace of God
as nothing.

[SC 3.V8.8 Brian Pickett, new translation]

༄༅

They tasted unholiness – they gulped down unholiness.

They did not think about God to know God's goodness, but only to life themselves above God, as if above a stranger.

They turned away from God's friendship with their own blazing pride, forgetting about God who is the ruling One.

[SCa, pp. 184, 185: 3.V1.14#]

In this vision –

Another beast was truly a grisly wolf.

This signifies those times when people will show their powers and success by committing a lot of robberies.

They will not show themselves as either black or white, but as grisly ones.

They will divide up the kingdoms.

Then the time will come when many souls are ensnared.

The error of errors will be lifted up, right up to heaven.

The gospel limps.

[SCa, p. 348: 3.VII. 6]

UNCERTAINTY – HELP!

Too much trust in myself, and distrust of God, leads to uncertainty.

In their uncertainty, people cry out for help.

The people in the battles were shouting again and again: 'Let us proceed to the heavens.' They stretch out to the mysteries of heaven, even though they are many times made weary by the craftiness of the devil. People were flung here and there.

[SCa, p. 170: 2.V7.15]

The people were very frightened. Indeed the people, shaking with great fear, said to each other: 'Alas, alas, what is this? Ach, we wretched ones, who will help us? Who will free us? For we do not know how we have been deceived. Let us turn back, let us turn back quickly to the testament of the Gospel of Christ. For, ach, ach, ach, we have been bitterly deceived.'

[SCa, p. 346: 3.VII]

ༀ

Nevertheless, with help from heaven, all of these people can be victorious. They place their hopes and good works with God.

[SCa, p. 170: 2.V7.15]

This faith has none of the uncertainty of unfaithfulness, because this faith did not found itself, but rather comes from a dependency on Christ.

[SCa, p. 32: 1.V3.11]

ༀ

Forgive us our sins according to your holiness, not according to our evil.

[SCa, p. 141: 2.V6.18]

Theme Nine: **Hazards and Trials**   **97**

Let us not forget,
that, as we are called to be saints,
so we are, by that very calling, called to suffer;
and, if we suffer, must not think it strange
concerning the fiery trial that is to try us;
nor be puffed up,
    by our privilege of suffering,
nor bring suffering needlessly upon us,
nor be eager to make out we have suffered for Christ,
    when we have but suffered for our faults, or not at all.

May God give us grace to act upon these rules,
    as well as to adopt and admire them;
and to say nothing for saying's sake,
    but to do much and say little!

John Henry Newman (1801–90)
Masters of Prayer, Church House Publishing, 1986, p. 20

SUFFERING

I, God, sometimes sustain people silently.

[SCa, p. 114: 2.V5.34]

My people have been protected by my willing them to be protected.

[SCa, p. 112: 2.V5.20]

※

If the very dark storms fall upon any person,
　　and this person has not consented to these with his or her heart,
　　with his or her will,
　　but nevertheless is still tormented –

If this person perseveres, then

　　　I will help this person quickly,
　　　and I will treasure this person as a friend.

He or she is able to overcome great difficulties because of love for me.

[SCa, p. 123: 2.V5.58]

※

In a time of great despair and desolation, God said to Mechthild of Magdeburg (1217–82):
　'I, God, am your playmate!
　I will lead the child in you in wonderful ways. I have chosen you!'

(Matthew Fox *Original Blessings*, p. 222)

God says:
　I know you are a frail vessel,
　but I want to communicate with you
　and be united to your sorrows.
　Supporting you, I will save you.

[SCa, p. 329: 3.V10.7]

※

For the Lord had a precious pearl which sunk down, falling into filth.
But the Lord, not allowing it to be in that filth, mercifully lifted it out and cleaned off the filth in which it had been lying – similar to the way that gold is cleaned in a furnace. And the Word took it back to its previous honour with *even greater glory*.

[SCa, p. 23: 1.V2.32]

Theme Nine: **Hazards and Trials** 　　　　　　　　　　　　　　　　　**99**

Do you not see how necessary
a World of Pains and troubles is
to school an Intelligence
and make it a soul?
A Place where the heart
must feel and suffer
in a thousand diverse ways.

John Keats, Letter to George and Georgina Keats, Spring 1819

It isn't that Christianity explains suffering, but it has a *use* for it.

Simone Weil

LIGHT HONOURED BY THE DARK

How could light be recognised except through darkness?
And how could darkness be known except through the radiant brightness
of my servants?

For light is honoured by darkness
and the part full of darkness
with its empty space
serves the part which is light.

[BDW 4.12 and 4.29; Brian Pickett, new translations]

※

Human beings ... behave like a bear in bodily pain.
The bear ... forces us to inner meekness, causing us to walk the right path
by exercising patience like a lamb, and to avoid evil by behaving as
cleverly as a serpent.
For through the distress of the body we often attain spiritual treasures through
which we come into possession of a higher kingdom.

[DWe, p. 44: V2.29]

※

O Spirit of burning ...
All creatures praise you
For they have this life from you.
You are the most precious ointment
For broken and septic wounds.
You change them into the most precious jewels.

[Ag, p. 97: SACR 18*]

THE DEAD WHO LIVE AND SILENCE:

Writing to God –

My dead remain hidden from me because they have entered into Your life.
They are conjoined with the jubilant song of Your endless love.

My dead live the unhampered and limitless Life that You live:
    they love with Your Love;
    and thus their love no longer fits into the frail and narrow frame
    of my present existence.

Their voice speaks in unison with Yours,
    trying to make itself heard above the noisy tumult of our incessant
    activity.

Against all this, their voice and Yours strive to enwrap us and all our words
    in Your eternal silence . . .

They are silent because they live, just as we chatter so loudly to try to make
    ourselves forget that we are dying . . .

By Your grace, O Lord, let it become ever more a life of faith in Your Light.

Karl Rahner, *Encounters with Silence*,
London, Sands & Co., 1960 p. 56

DEATH

The soul gives life to the body as fire gives light to darkness.
Therefore O human, you are not just a bundle of marrow!

[SCb, p. 120: 1.V4.18]

The soul leads the person to full usefulness.

[SCa, p. 51: 1.V4.17]

All things are understood through the soul as through a master: the soul investigates
things in the same way that wheat is separated from the chaff.
It enquires whether things are –
useful or useless,
lovable or hateful, or
whether they relate to life or death.

[SCa, p. 51: 1.V4.19]

⁑

When the soul extracts itself from the body, it leaves behind its relationship to the
body . . .

[SCa, p. 57: 1.V4, 29#]

When it has thus freed itself, there come certain spirits, some of light and some of
darkness, who have been its life's companions.

[SCb, p. 125: 1.V4.29]

They expect resolution, after the soul has untied itself from the body.

[SCa, p. 57: 1.V4.29]

⁑

They lead it where the Celestial Judge will judge it on the merit of its deeds.
The choirs of angels sing 'You are just, O Lord!', because God's justice has no flaw in it.
No smear of dung soils the sun, and likewise no wickedness of injustice can touch
God.
Therefore, evil must be thrown down . . . and good embraced in love of life.

God knows what good you are capable of.

God wishes from the beginning to the end of the world to take pleasure in His elect,
that they may be faithfully crowned, adorned with the brightness of virtue.

God is good

[SCb, p. 125, 126: 1.V4.29/30*]

Theme Ten:

Resources

Illustration overleaf:
*Touched by the Holy Spirit . . . you will be intoxicated with Charity . . .
of joyful face and cheerful look.*

THE HOLY SPIRIT AND VIRTUE

Wherever Humility seized the serpent, it very quickly shattered the serpent as if it were a worthless thread.

[SCa, p. 24: 1.V2.33]

⁂

God says:
To the person who voluntarily receives the seed of my word with a good heart, I superabundantly allot the great gifts of the Holy Spirit.

[SCa, p. 324: 3.V10.4]

⁂

You are made wealthy with virtues.

[SCa, p. 331: 3.V10.9]

⁂

The *virtues*,
who have been touched healthfully by the Holy Spirit,
are of joyful face,
and cheerful look.

[SCa, p. 332: 5.V10.14, 9]

⁂

I kindle the strongest virtues within you, who are intensely lovable to me: as a result you will be intoxicated with charity.

[SCa, p. 143: 2.V6.21]

Therefore it is needful that thou look straight with the eyes of thy spirit to God, as straight as a cable stretches taut from a ship to her anchor. Then, as the anchor is fixed firmly in the earth, so do thou fasten thine eyes to God. Even though the ship tosses at sea in the waves, yet she is safe and unbroken as long as her cable holds fast to her anchor.
And with these anchors

   – wisdom and humility
   and prudence and moderation
   and justice and mercy
   and reason and maturity of mind
   and goodwill and cleanness and abstinence –

with these thou shalt fasten firmly to God the cable that shall keep safe the ship of thy soul.

King Alfred the Great, 849–901,
interpreting St Augustine

THE VIRTUES

According to Hildegard, life from God was transmitted into the plants, animals, and precious gems. People, in turn, ate the plants and animals, and acquired some of the gems, thereby obtaining *viriditas* (the greenness/growth/principle of life).

People then gave out *viriditas* through the *virtues*, hence their importance in the chain of being.

[SCa, p. xxvii, Introduction]

A faithful person should leave the foolishness of infancy behind and should ascend to the fullness of the virtues.

[SCa, p. 93: 2.V2.9]

The Virtues speak:

But we virtues have been placed against the cunning and bragging which the devil sends out into the world to swallow up souls.

All the craftiness of the devil is led to nothing through us, for he is confused from every direction.

> *God will be known through us.*
> *God ought not to be hidden.*

[SCa, p. 308: 3.V9.2]

Wisdom is with the highest God before every creature.

[SCa, p. 312: 3.V9.25]

Wisdom says:

When you started to run on the way to God, there were gnats and flies buzzing with their loud noise as a hindrance to you.

But you took the fan of inspiration of the Holy Spirit and drove the gnats and flies away from yourselves.

The fan of the inspiration of the Holy Spirit hastened to you, and there was help from God.

[SCa, p. 307: 3.V9.1]

Thereupon the sky got very bright and I heard all the virtues sing in a wondrous manner to the various types of music.

They persisted strongly in the way of truth as they sang the praises of celestial joy.

They persisted strongly as they called those with complaints back to praising with joy.

And they persisted in exhorting and encouraging themselves so that they might fight back the snares of the devil and help people gain salvation.

And the sound was that of the voice of a multitude singing a musical performance with harmony, in praise of the celestial order.

[SCa, p. 375: 3.13]

This ninth vision in the third part of *Scivias* has some very powerful resonances with our modern psychology. It is worth going through carefully.

> The right head – the 'Root of the Good' – looks to the middle head and says: 'I took root in the first beginning on the mountain of a high summit, namely God. Therefore, O Holiness, since you are able to stand, it is proper that I cling to you'.
>
> And the left head – 'Not Refraining from Self' – looks to the middle head and says (in a manner that takes quite a bit of deciphering!):
>
> 'O alas, alas, alas, how rigid and inflexible I am. I can overcome myself only with much difficulty. If I flee to you for help, O Holiness, why are you still nevertheless *not able to stand separate without my help*? Ach, ach, ach, the neglect! It behooves me to root out a troublesome thorn which tries to drive me to destruction by fighting against me. I must dig this thorn out before it sinks into me completely and before it festers in me as a decaying dead body. O Holiness, just as you are able to persevere freely, I want to shatter the devil with the one true God.'
>
> [SCa, p. 310: 3.v9.4, 5, 6]

That really does make one think . . .

Is *my* thorn an attitude, a prejudice, a resentment?

Or perhaps it is a compulsion I have grown used to since childhood?

What is it that is 'driving' my actions?

Are these things compatible with holiness – do they have to be 'dug out'?

How do they relate to the 'first beginning', either my own, or the first principles of life?

Hildegard has given us some profound food for thought in her three-headed image of Holiness.

It is useful to put this part of Hildegard's vision next to St Paul's requests to God to remove his mysterious thorn of the flesh (2 Cor. 12:7).

HOLINESS AND CHOICE

Holiness – together with the *joy of life* –
is known in the soul without any indignation of shame.

In my vision she had three heads:

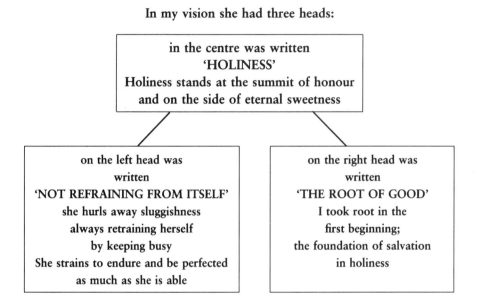

in the centre was written
'HOLINESS'
Holiness stands at the summit of honour
and on the side of eternal sweetness

on the left head was
written
'NOT REFRAINING FROM ITSELF'
she hurls away sluggishness
always retraining herself
by keeping busy
She strains to endure and be perfected
as much as she is able

on the right head was
written
'THE ROOT OF GOOD'
I took root in the
first beginning;
the foundation of salvation
in holiness

The head in the middle looked at the other two heads, and they looked at the middle head. All the heads brought their own *usefulness* together in turn. This signifies that they strongly agree with their inner vision when they need to make a choice. But not one of them is strong enough to endure without the help of the other two, in order to bring people to perfection.

[SCa, p. 318: 3.V9.29]

Tune me
O Lord,
Into one harmony with thee,
One full responsive vibrant chord,
Unto Thy praise, all love and melody.
Tune me, O Lord.

Christina Rossetti, 1830–94

HARMONY

Harmony provides a greater brightness in the human soul
than the mortal mind, weighed down with a frail body,
can ever grasp.

To those who commit themselves to the sweat of just labour,
in prosperity or adversity,
her power extends the protection of her shining goodness.

Because of her love of God,
she avoids the clashes and the splits of the faithless
and pants for the vision of perpetual peace.

[SC 3.V10.27, Brian Pickett, new translation]

※

The blessed spirits
bring forth the very greatest happiness
in indescribable sounds.

[SCa, p. 73: 3.V6.11]

Hildegard is passionately keen on people making the most use of their 'ration-ality', or 'speculative knowledge', in order to make good choices. She says we have been supplied with the means to make these choices, even in the face of ferocious evil, but we are not left on our own. We also have the Virtues to bolster and scaffold us.

To Hildegard, the Virtues are not part of us, to be claimed by us and taken as personal merits. They are there, beside us, to be called upon and *used* by us. To 'use', 'to be used', 'usefulness' and 'uselessness' are terms that are of primary importance in Hildegard's work.

Words change, as attitudes and cultures change down the centuries. Is there something of great value in the concept of making use of virtues as tools, as we carve out our way towards God? Something that has got lost in the undergrowth, as our fascination with self-development and self-autonomy has grown?

How true is it to me, that there are things 'outside myself', tools supplied by my Creator, left around for me to reach out for?

Or do I believe I only have my own internal resources to rely on?

And for those with whom I come into contact – those I live with, or work with, or work for – if among them there are people whose 'internal resources' are shrivelled or damaged, is there anything they can call upon to come over onto their side?

What ways can I, being who I am, put into effect what I have noted down here?

SPEAKERS AND TOOLS

Speakers are the makers of spices,
 like fruits which offer a sweet savour to those who taste them,
 for they prove themselves sweet to people
 by the usefulness of their office.

As the sun, who is my Son, dances in the flesh,
 the light of the holy Gospel shines in His preaching
  – pouring forth from Him and His disciples –
to be a fruit of blessing.

       [SC 2.V5.37 and 3.V4.10, Brian Pickett, new translations]

         ❧

Tools

The three tools by which the Church seeks the eternal in her sons and daughters are:
 the nourishment from her teachers;
 the fight of the faithful against the devil;
 and the turning of the faithful away from any consent to evil.

        [SC3.V9.26, Brian Pickett, new translation]

GOD LOVETH, THAT HE MIGHT *BE* LOVE.

Love proceedeth from itself, for unless it be of itself it is not love.

Where Love is the Lover
Love streaming from the Lover is the Lover
and the Lover streaming from Himself and existing in another person.

God loveth that He might be Love.
Infinitely delightful to all objects,
Infinitely delighted in all, and
Infinitely pleased in Himself, for being infinitely delightful to all.
All this He attaineth by Love.

The soul is shrivelled up and buried in a grave that does not love.
All hyperboles are but little pigmies in comparison of the Truth.

You are prone to love as the sun is to shine;
By Love our souls are married and soldered to the all;
We must love them infinitely, but in God, and for God, and God in them.

We should be all *life* and *mettle* and *vigour* and *LOVE* to everything,
And that would poise us.

Thomas Traherne, 1636–74 *Centuries*: selections from 42–68

LOVE

Love overflows into all
Glorious from ocean's depths beyond the farthest star
Bounteous in loving all creation.

[Ag, p. 31: SACR 16]

✠

For, though the cherubim and seraphim fear to look on you
    in the almighty power of your heavenly majesty,
You let a poor woman touch the fringe of your garment
    when you wore your earthly body.
And so, at once she received her health again
    for she had found the true fount of tender-heartedness.

[Ag, p. 52: GB 28]

✠

How wonderful is your kindness, O God,
How amazing your tenderheartedness
    revered by the angels in Heaven!
Sinners find trust to seek you in every need and trouble
    and implore your tender heart.

[Ag, p. 53: GB 29]

✠

O eternal God,
Let your love for us burn within you;
You first made us to be in your love
When you begot your Son at the dawn of time
Before creation was made . . .
Lead us to the joy of your salvation.

[Ag, p. 102: SACR 2]

Theme Eleven:

Meditation

Illustration overleaf:
Take a rest in the strength of the Holy Spirit.

REST

The teachers of the church, steeped with the gifts of the Holy Spirit, take a
rest in the strength of the Holy Spirit.

[SCa, p. 314: 3.V11.26]

On the seventh day of quietness
the seventh day is one of rest.

[SCa, p. 351: 3.V11.23]

All shall be Amen and Alleluia:
We shall rest and we shall see
We shall see and we shall know
We shall know and we shall understand
We shall love and we shall praise
Behold our end which is no end.

St Augustine of Hippo, died 430 AD

Our Lord God shewed that it is full great pleasure to Him
that a silly soul come to Him naked, plainly, and homely.

For then God enfolds us, He wraps us, clasps us, and becloseth us,
that He may never leave us.

For our soul sitteth in God in very Rest;
our soul standeth in God in very strength; and
our soul is rooted in God in endless love.

And soothly I saw that into this high deepness our Good Lord Himself leadeth
us.

And I saw that Our Lord sitteth in the soul, even-right in peace and rest.
And this was a singular joy and bliss to me that I saw Him sitting: for the
sureness of sitting sheweth endless dwelling.

Dame Julian, Revelations, chs. 67, 68 and elsewhere, 1413 AD

❦

In all creation,
There is nothing so like God as stillness.

Meister Eckhart, 1260–1327

GOD RESTED

God finds rest
in the faith
which God has helped provide –
just as a great lord is touched by the throne on which he sits.

[SCa, p. 180: 3.V1.2]

Having worked for six days, God rested on the seventh.

[SCa, p. 336: 3.V10.15]

The Holiness and Goodness of God is *gleamed* through the complete Word.

[SCa, p. 81: 2.V1.4]

God and the breath
With every breeze, I awaken everything to life.
The air lives by turning green and being in bloom.
The waters flow as if they were alive.
The winds have subordinate wings, with gentle power, so they do not become
    dangerous.
In the same way the body envelopes the soul and maintains it so that the soul
    does not blow away.
The breath of the soul strengthens and fortifies the body so that it does not
    disappear.
Thus I remain hidden in every kind of reality as a fiery power.

[DWe, p. 92: V1.2]

I am the supreme and fiery force who has kindled all sparks of life.
I, the fiery life,
    blaze in the beauty of the fields,
        shine in the waters, and
            burn in the sun, moon and stars.
I bring all things to life;
I breathe in them all, because I am life.

[DWf, p. 143: LDO V1.ch. 2]

Man is continually moved by his breath, as the fire contains the nimble flame.
I, having the wind of the resounding Word, have breathed into all things.
All living things take their radiance from me;
I am the life that remains the same through eternity.
Eternity is called the Father,
    the Word is called the Son,
        and the breath that connects these two is called the Holy Spirit.

[DWc, p. 92: V1.2*]

BREATHING

The soul inhales the breath of life into the body,
    and then expels it.
By exhaling, the fire of the organism is diminished,
    and warmth is removed.
If warmth were not discharged from the body,
    the fire of the soul might burn the body;
just as a house might be completely destroyed
    by the heat of a fire.

Through the fiery capacity of the soul,
    we are also able to realize that we possess God.
Through the breath of the Spirit we understand that
    we can act within our body.

The power of the soul clothes us with flesh and blood
    and completes us as a total unity;
just as all the fruits of the Earth are ripened
    by the blowing of the wind.

[DWe, p. 125: V4.103]

Meditation has nothing to do with edification.
It is, rightly understood, a matter of life and death.
The intention is always to make possible a religious experience and to
    confirm and deepen it.
One revolves around the *Supra-Mundane*, the Divine Being –
    around *God*.

It is a matter of finding anchorage, rootedness;
in the anchoring in this other dimension there is a strong development
    of the power of love.

It is for those who experience a need, a profound unrest,
    a feeling of there being something in me, a very deep inner core
in which the sclerosed patches of the soul can, very gradually,
    slowly begin to be recognised,
    and be rendered supple again.

It is a matter of transformation,
    in which we become capable more and more,
    of letting this other dimension work through us:
    of becoming transparent to transcendence.

Durkheim; Frankfurter Vorträge – 1, pp. 237–8; 38–9

RECEIVING DEEPLY

Receiving more deeply
that
you may reveal more openly.

[SCa, p. 45: 1.V4.9]

❧

It behooves you, every hour,
to think about the ways you can make
this grand gift useful
for yourself
and for others.

[SCa, p. 331: 3.V10.9]

Hildegard and Durkheim both came from the same geographical area but they are separated by seven centuries.

It's all very well that advanced spiritual explorers like them should tell us that meditation is something to be considered every hour, and that it is a matter of life and death; but can *I* do it in *my* life as I live it *now*? Is it an idea I take to? Enough to put a time and a place aside for it?

For the beginner, there are a great many books with practical hints about how to start. Shall I decide to look out for one, to borrow or buy one? When? Where from?

There are an increasing number of small home-based groups that practise silent prayer or meditation. The Christian-based ones may be often linked to the Julian Meetings, or Servants of Christ the King, or the John Main Christian Meditation Centre, or simply attached to a local church. Addresses of those in your area can be obtained from the contacts listed at the end of the book.

Am I going to decide to follow one of these up? If so, *when*?

Some people like to start an adventure like this with a friend, some prefer to do it on their own; who would I approach about it, if I wanted to talk it over?

Basically, it's about clearing the clutter, *letting go*, and *letting God*.

IMMEASURABLE GLORY

God is full of immeasurable glory
and no one can be sated with the sweetness of God.

[SC 3.V10.11]

☫

Therefore extend yourself in the fountain of abundance.

[SC 1.V1 introduction, Brian Pickett, new translations]

Theme Twelve:

The Day of the Great Revelation

Illustration overleaf:
Be ablaze with enthusiasm . . . an alive, burning offering before God.

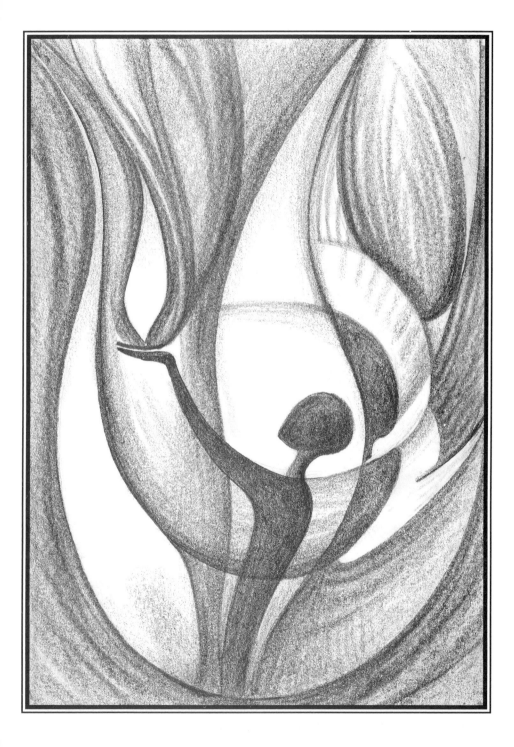

RISING UP

The world, which is curved, is pressed down with so many hardships and calamities that it can bring about its own end with its own powers . . . (!).

But my bride – however weary – cannot be destroyed in any way, however much she is attacked.

She will rise up,
stronger and more powerful,
more beautiful,
more bright.

[SCa, p. 46: 3.V11.1]

❧

For I am that love which neither blazing pride casts down,
nor the deepest fall tears to pieces,
nor the breadth of evil rubs away.

Do not refuse to listen.

[SCa, p. 394: 3.V13.16]

All thing that Our Lord hath ordained to do,
    it is His will that we pray therefore
    either in special, or in general.

For prayer is a right wise understanding of that fulness of joy that is to come;

    * with well-longing . . . overcoming against all our weakness
    * and sure trust . . . overcoming all our doubtful dreads

For he saith – *I am the ground of Thy beseeching*
    and all that faileth us we shall find in Him.

        So is He worshipped, and we sped.

                Dame Julian, *Revelations** # ch. 42

FOULNESS VANISHING

Whatever is foul in the world will vanish, as if it had never been – just as salt
dissolves when it has been put into water.

[SCa, p. 367: 3.V12.2]

Like night ceasing to be when it has been broken up by the heat of the sun.

[SCa, p. 371: 3.V12.12]

※

The greatest quietness of Tranquillity now rises up as part of the divine plan.

[SCa, p. 371: 3.V12.12]

※

There,
    praises of jubilation,
        simplicity of agreement,
            and love to the faithful,
                passed through me.

[SCa, p. 392: 3.V13.14]

※

A musical performance, which softens hard hearts and casts forth all the
shadows of darkness – making those things pure and light which had
been concealed – offers unwearied praises faithfully to God.

[SCa, p. 392: 3.V13.15]

The Word will appear as terrible to the unjust
  as caressing to the just.

[SCa, p. 369: 3.V12.6]

Whoever understands God through faith,
let this one rejoice incessantly in God with faithful devotion,
. . . having been poured over with the Spirit of depth and of height.

[SCa, p. 392: 3.V13.15]

THE HOLY TRINITY

It is God the Father
who, before all ages
begat God's one fruitful Word,
gloriously flowering in the Virgin.

The Word went forth from the Father
on a spiritual exodus,
and returned again in the fruitfulness of the flesh.

From the Father and the Word
the Holy Spirit proceeded
with fiery vigour, fresh as greenery,
and hallowed the waters;
moving over their face like an innocent bird,
and drenched the apostles
with the heat of fire.

Power, Will and *Heat*:

These three are peaks on the one summit of their working.
In the power lies the will,
in the will the heat,
and they are as inseparable as the breath of a person breathing out.
Three persons
one with each other inseparably working together.

[SC 3.V7.8–10; Brian Pickett, new translation]

Hildegard of Bingen once said that *singing* words reveals their true meaning directly to the soul through bodily vibrations. I think we can conclude from this statement that her world-view centres around an intimate relationship between body (the mouth, throat, vocal chords, diaphragm, and lungs) and the spirit (breath).

The goal of creation for Hildegard is that all creatures sing with one voice the same praises.

Hildegard's compositions are incredibly physical. This makes wonderful sense if we realise that she was a physical scientist as well as a musician. Singing her music comes close to hyperventilation at times. When she writes about the Spirit, you know she understands the Spirit as wind, as breath, because you become the wind. When she writes about Divine Mysteries, you sing out of the deepest space of your physical being from the comfort of the normal range to the extremes of your potential.

Here music reveals that we, too, are divine mysteries.

Hildegard's melodies are as memorable to me as a melody from Mozart or Mahler – romantic in their wholeness and
vast in their expansiveness.
Her music is unique for its time and, I am tempted to say,
for any time.

Brendan Doyle
[DWe pp. 364–5, introduction to the *Songs of Hildegard*]

O ETERNAL VIGOUR!

All the world has found its order in your heart.
Through your Word all things have been created,
     as you willed.
Your own Word even clothed itself in flesh,
     in the same form which came from Adam.
And thus that same human clothing has been cleansed
     from the greatest pain.

O how great is the compassion of the Saviour,
     who has set all the world free by taking our flesh!
This grace Divinity breathed forth
     without the chains of sin,
And thus that same human clothing has been cleansed
     from the greatest pain.

Glory to the Father, and to the Son, and to the Holy Spirit.
And thus that same human clothing has been cleansed
     from the greatest pain.

[SACR 58, Brian Pickett, new translation]

So this is the final extract from the works of Hildegard of Bingen to be offered in this volume. These selections have been like gifts, gems gathered out of mammoth quarries presented to us by one of the most remarkable women of all time, Hildegard of Bingen.

Maybe the reader's appetite has been whetted for more of Hildegard's work; it has to be said that all authorities comment on the difficulty of separating the gems from the material in which they are embedded. Because there was plenty of time and labour to take the dictation of all her words, the ideas and images, her metaphors and accompanying similes, come tumbling onto the page in a confusion of colours and variety. Most of the readily available translations of her work – some of them the original 'quarry' and some of them extracts – are listed in the bibliography at the end of this book.

It may be that not all the selections offered here have moved every reader. But at this end stage it is useful to run back over the way we have come and pick out what has spoken most keenly and positively for *you*, as an individual.

- Was it the intensity of the passion of Hildegard for God and His *Viriditas?*
- Did the images of evil and the reality for Hildegard of Lucifer, strike home?
- Was it the sobering notion that our own resources, our own zeal, by themselves are never sufficient?
- Maybe the idea of being surrounded by the scaffolding of Virtues was comforting? Hildegard would expect this also to be empowering.
- It could be that the activity of receiving, breathing in the Spirit, becoming re-saturated, will be strong enough to enable you to experience more of it in a deliberate, chosen way. Hildegard is very hot on *choice*!

In this space here, you may like to make a note of the page numbers you would like to reread at some stage – the places you would look to *first*, when you pick up the book next time.

And then continue on your way, enriched by carrying with you at least some of these gifts from Hildegard.

Be not lax in celebrating.
Be not lazy in the festive service of God.
Be ablaze with enthusiasm.
Let us be an alive, burning, offering before the altar of God.
[SCd, p. 93 and 115 – quoted from Uhlein, p. 128: 3.V13]

ACKNOWLEDGEMENTS

Personal Help
What could I have done without it!

My thanks are due, firstly, to Hebe Wellbourne from the Elsie Briggs House of Prayer in Bristol who – perhaps unknowingly! – started the search for me;

to Jane Williams, of the University of Trinity College, Bristol, who encouraged me;

to Brian Pickett, priest, who kept me on the right path;

to Colin Morris, Professor of Medieval History at Southampton University, who pointed me to unfamiliar texts;

to Mamie Bruce-Gardyne, of the Kirkton of Airlie by Kirriemuir, who so scrupulously checked every reference for me;

to David Moloney, my publisher's warmly efficient editor, who brought the book to fruition;

to Sister Mary Stephen Grindon-Welch, from the Canonesses of the Holy Sepulchre, near Chelmsford. It has been her inspiration which fired the illustrations, published here for the first time; they light up the words of Hildegard for all of us.

Last but by no means least, to my husband Trevor, our four daughters and six grandchildren, who so patiently put up with my periodic withdrawal – at times when that was the last thing they wanted!

My deepest thanks and unqualified appreciation to all of them; I have indeed been favoured in the process of producing this book.

In addition to the main sources listed on p. xxix, the following are gratefully acknowledged:

Julian of Norwich's Revelations of Divine Love, edited by Dom Hudleston, Burns and Oates Ltd, 1927

John V. Taylor, for permission to quote his unpublished poem 'The Angels'

The Edge of Glory: Prayers in the Celtic Tradition, by David Adam, London, SPCK, 1985

FURTHER READING

For details of the main sources of the works of Hildegard from which the quotations in this book have been selected, please refer to p. xxix.

Bowie, Fiona, *Beguine Spirituality*, London, SPCK, 1989.

Colman O'Dell, M. 'Elisabeth of Schonau and Hildegard of Bingen: Prophets of the Lord', in *Medieval Religious Women*, Vol. Two, *Peace Weavers*, London, Cistercian Publications Inc., Mowbrays, 1987.

Derolez, Albert, 'The Genesis of Hildegard of Bingen's "Liber Divinorum Operum" – the Codicological Evidence' in Gumbert and Haan (eds.) *Litterae Textuales* Vol. 2, pp. 23–33, Amsterdam, Van Gendt, 1972.

Durka, Gloria, *Praying with Hildegard of Bingen*, Minnesota, St Mary's Press, 1991.

Fox, Matthew, *Original Blessing*, Santa Fe, Bear & Co., 1983.

Grant, Patrick, *A Dazzling Darkness: an Anthology of Western Mysticism*, London, Fount Paperbacks, 1985.

Newman, Barbara, *Sister of Wisdom: St Hildegard's Theology of the Feminine*, Berkeley CA, University of California Press, 1987.

'Divine Power Made Perfect in Weakness: St Hildegard on the Frail Sex' in *Medieval Religious Women*, Vol. Two, *Peace Weavers*, London, Cistercian Publications Inc., Mowbrays, 1987.

Uhlein, Gabriele, *Meditations with Hildegard of Bingen*, Santa Fe, Bear & Co., 1983.